MASS-PARTICIPATORY ECONOMY

MASS-PARTICIPATORY ECONOMY

A Democratic Alternative for Korea

Kim Dae Jung

Published by

 Center for International Affairs
Harvard University

and

 University Press of America

Co-published by arrangement with the
Center for International Affairs, Harvard University

The Center for International Affairs provides a forum for the
expression of responsible views. It does not, however, necessarily
agree with them.

The Center For International Affairs Executive Committee, 1984–85

Samuel P. Huntington, *Eaton Professor of the Science of Government; Director, Center for International Affairs*

Lisa Anderson, *Director of Student Programs; Assistant Professor of Government*

Leslie H. Brown, *Director of the Fellows Program*

Seyom Brown, *Acting Director, University Consortium for Research on North America*

Richard N. Cooper, *Maurits C. Boas Professor of International Economics*

Paul M. Doty, *Mallinckrodt Professor of Biochemistry; Director, Center for Science and International Affairs*

Stephan Haggard, *Acting Director of Student Programs; Assistant Professor of Government*

Chester D. Haskell, *Executive Officer*

Douglas A. Hibbs, *Professor of Government*

Stanley Hoffmann, *C. Douglas Dillon Professor of the Civilization of France; Chairman, Center for European Studies*

Herbert Kelman, *Richard Clarke Cabot Professor of Social Ethics*

Joseph S. Nye, *Clarence Dillon Professor of International Affairs*

Dwight H. Perkins, *Harold Hitchings Burbank Professor of Political Economy; Director, Harvard Institute for International Development*

Robert D. Putnam, *Chairman, Department of Government; Professor of Government*

Louise Richardson, *Ph.D. Candidate in Government*

Sidney Verba, *Director of the University Library; Carl H. Pforzheimer University Professor*

Ezra Vogel, *Director, Program on U.S. – Japan Relations; Professor of Sociology*

The Center for International Affairs is a multidisciplinary research institution within Harvard University. Founded in 1958, the Center seeks to provide a stimulating environment for a diverse group of scholars and practitioners studying various aspects of international affairs. Its purpose is the development and dissemination of knowledge concerning the basic subjects and problems of international relations. Major Center research programs include national security affairs, U.S. relations with Europe, Japan, Africa, and other areas of the world, nonviolent sanctions in conflict and defense, international economic policy, and other critical issues. At any given time, over 160 individuals are working at the Center, including faculty members from Harvard and neighboring institutions, practitioners of international affairs, visiting scholars, research associates, post-doctoral fellows, and graduate and undergraduate student associates.

Contents

Preface

I have long been in opposition to the South Korean governments of Rhee Syngman, Park Chung Hee, and Chun Doo Hwan, mainly because my faith in democracy and desire to bring it about in my country clashed with their dictatorial aims. Because of my philosophical disagreement with these leaders, I have developed counterproposals to address fundamental aspects of their policies. Where I disagree with my opponents, I have always presented practical alternatives and avoided unconstructive criticisms. Thus, during my campaign for the presidency in 1971, I presented my economic development program in a book, proposed peaceful dialogue and exchange with North Korea as a first step toward reunification, and suggested that the four superpowers (the United States, the Soviet Union, the People's Republic of China, and Japan) get involved in the peace and unification process in order to make it feasible and durable.

Because I advocated peaceful dialogue and exchange with North Korea, I was immediately accused of dancing to the tune of North Korean leader Kim Il Sung, and the other part of my unification policy proposal was dismissed as being impractical, naive, and worse. Shortly after the election, however, President Park adopted my proposal for a North–South dialogue and claimed the idea as his own. I fully supported him in that endeavor. Unfortunately, the reunification talks went nowhere, because both governments used them to shore up their own positions in domestic politics and were not really interested in reunification. Recently, I could not help feeling some sense of justification as the idea of reunification talks involving one or more of the four superpowers has been put forward as a real possibility and is being seriously discussed. I do not claim that my idea was thirteen years ahead of its time; rather, we have wasted fourteen years and are likely to waste more because the rulers of both parts of the Korean peninsula have been more interested in manipulating the unification issue to preserve their own power structures than in peacefully reunifying the nation.

My economic development program was also maliciously criticized as being anti-business and pro-labor, a veiled attempt to label my policy socialistic. Nevertheless, election returns showed that I garnered 46 percent of the total votes despite manipulation of the results and intimidation practiced by government forces at polling places. Readers of this book will easily find out why the Korean people rejected the accusation that my policies are anti-business. I will show that my opposition to the economic policies of Park Chung Hee and Chun Doo Hwan is based on my conviction that I have better alternatives, and will present positions for discussion among interested people.

The Republic of Korea, or South Korea (hereafter referred to as Korea), has long been recognized as one of America's most dependable allies and a bulwark against communism. The Korean–American relationship, which was centered on mutual interests in security until the mid-1960s, has had an additional dimension since then as the volume of mutual trade expanded. Currently, forty thousand American troops are stationed in Korea, and the Korean–American relationship is expected to become increasingly important to America's global security. Peace and stability in East Asia depend critically on the stability of the Korean peninsula, which cannot be maintained without full participation of the Korean people in the enjoyment of the fruits of economic development. Thus, for security reasons alone, Korea's economic development with social justice is an important matter to the United States.

The economic dimension of Korean–American relations has become an important issue in its own right. Korea is now America's eighth-largest trading partner, and the United States is Korea's largest export market. A healthy and dynamic economy in Korea will thus assure the United States a stable and growing trading partner.

Korea's political and economic problems are in many ways similar to those of other Third World countries. Oppressive and corrupt governments backed by military forces, huge gaps between the rich and the poor, crushing foreign-debt burdens, and excessive government interference with market functions are commonly found, in varying degrees, in most Third World nations. These countries are America's ideological battlegrounds against the Soviet Union. The United States has done poorly in this battle and is not likely to fare any better in the future unless its Third World policies are based on a better understanding of their problems. I hope this book will help Americans understand these problems better.

One may wonder why this book is needed. To many Western observers, Korea's economic development seems enviable, and they may feel it is absurd to consider any *alternative* development strategy at all. But such misunderstanding is precisely why this book is needed. Many books have been written to show how well the Korean economy has been growing or why it has been so successful, but the dark side of the Korean economy has not been examined.

For example, Korea's foreign debt at the end of 1983 was the fourth-largest in the world and very close to that of number three, Argentina. Yet the American press has not paid much attention to this problem, compared with its coverage of the same problem in the Latin American countries. Foreign debt is only one of many serious problems facing the Korean economy. The huge and growing gaps among income classes, regions, and economic sectors, and ever-worsening social injustice, including brutal oppression of workers, created social unrest that led to the 1979 riots and the assassination of President Park. After the violent takeover of the government in May 1980, General Chun Doo Hwan was able to clamp a lid on this problem for a short period of time. However, social discontent has been brewing, and recently student protests have greatly increased. There had never been social stability under the Park Chung Hee regime, and there is even less stability now.

Unless these social, political, and economic problems are recognized and solved soon, there will be more violent upheavals in Korea, and the United States may lose not only a large export market but also one of its most dependable allies. I hope to offer in this book an alternative development strategy that I believe will benefit not only the Korean people but also, in the long run, the United States as well.

1

Introduction

Economic growth vs. economic development

Western observers have generally viewed economic growth in South Korea during the past two decades as a "success story." Sometimes referred to as a member of the Asian "Gang of Four" (the others are Taiwan, Hong Kong, and Singapore), Korea indeed enjoyed one of the world's highest rates of growth. Its per capita rate of growth in gross national product (GNP) (7.1 percent per year from 1960 to 1979) was surpassed only by the People's Democratic Republic of Yemen (11.8 percent), the Yemen Arab Republic (10.9 percent), Rumania (9.2 percent), and Singapore (7.4 percent).[1] As a result, the Korean government's economic policy has been touted as an example of "enlightened management," and many development economists have studied the causes of Korea's success to determine whether the Korean experience could be duplicated elsewhere.[2]

I am proud of my people for such spectacular accomplishments, achieved despite the stifling presence of the all-powerful government and its mismanagement of the economy. However, I believe the Korean government has been given more credit for the so-called success than it really deserves. Behind the facade of rapidly growing exports and aggregate production level, serious imbalances—between industrial sectors, between regions, among income groups, and between large and small firms—have emerged during the past two decades, and these imbalances are worsening each year. Unless these imbalances are corrected, *growth* in aggregate output alone will not bring about economic *development* in Korea. According to economists William Loehr and John Powelson:

> Economic development is the process by which a society (however defined) achieves greater material wealth and more equitable distribution of wealth among its members. The *participation* [italics added] of all groups (however defined) in both the production and decision-making arenas is a goal in its own right, except for those whose omission is either by necessity or by social agreement, such as the aged, the infirm, and children.[3]

Thus, Korea's rapid economic growth, which has not been accompanied by participation of all groups in economic, social, and political decision making, cannot be viewed as economic development. Moreover,

1

continuation of the existing trends will soon lead to serious economic and political crises. My program for a *Mass-Participatory Economy* in Korea is based on my conviction that participation of all groups under a democratic political system is the only way to achieve genuine and lasting economic development.

The goal of my program

In 1971 I presented, as a democratic alternative to Park Chung Hee's almost command-style economic policy, an economic development program aimed at alleviating the sense of alienation among the masses and promoting their full participation in all aspects of the economic development process.[4] The world and Korean economies have changed a great deal since then, but I believe the policy approaches of my 1971 book are still appropriate and sound. The goal of my program was, and still remains, a proper balance among three major objectives: growth (efficiency), equitable distribution of income, and price stability. These three objectives often conflict with one another.[5] Because a unilateral imposition of one leader's preference can only result in public discontent, the three objectives must be balanced by full participation of the masses. That is the goal of my program for Mass-Participatory Economy.

Growth

Economic growth is a necessary condition for economic development. Growth can be achieved by increasing the *quantity* of inputs, improving the *quality* of inputs, and by using inputs efficiently. Quantity and quality of inputs are important factors of growth, but inefficient use of a large quantity of high-quality inputs will result in waste. Thus, efficient use of resources is the most important element of economic growth.

Although the Korean economy has benefited from a well-educated and highly disciplined labor force, this quality advantage has been offset to a large extent by the counterproductive anti-labor policy of the Park and Chun regimes. The resulting inefficiencies have been overcome by sufficiently increasing the quantity of inputs.[6] To increase the quantity of inputs, the Park and Chun regimes have had to borrow heavily from abroad, earning a dubious distinction as the fourth-largest debtor nation in the world. Had the resources been efficiently used, Korea would not have been so heavily indebted to foreign banks. My program would rely less on borrowing and more on encouraging foreign direct investment. However, foreign investors should not be given special privileges beyond those allowed to domestic investors; both foreign and domestic investors must operate under the same rules.

Improvement in the quality of inputs is becoming increasingly more important as the world economy is rapidly moving into a high-technology era. To catch up with the fast-moving developed countries, therefore, a strong emphasis must be given to education, research and development, and labor productivity enhancement. Education improves the quality of labor and thus permits the introduction of advanced technologies. Labor productivity can be increased, in the short run, by using better equipment. But, in the long run, cooperative labor–management relations are the key to productivity growth.

The Korean economy under the Park and Chun regimes has been plagued by inefficient allocation of valuable resources. The inefficiency has been the result of government interference in almost every aspect of market functions, including pricing, credit allocation, industrial location decisions, and labor–management relations. This interference has left the Korean economy in a state of serious imbalance. The imbalances between the manufacturing sector and the agricultural sector, between large conglomerates and small or medium-sized firms, between the export sector and the domestic-market-oriented sector, between the urban and rural economies, between regions, and between the rich and the poor are serious and ever-growing. Thus, a cornerstone of my program will be to restore market functions free of government interference and to allow all groups—entrepreneurs, workers, farmers, and consumers—to take full advantage of the opportunities provided by the free market.

Equitable distribution of income

The fruits of economic development and the sacrifices required for a successful development program must be fairly distributed. It betrays the purpose of economic development to concentrate government favors within a small group of people and firms, to interfere unfairly with the credit allocation function of the financial institutions for the benefit of the privileged, and to favor a particular region over others. Regional favoritism in the allocation of investment projects is particularly damaging to national unity.

Unless Korea's huge gap between the rich and the poor is corrected in the near future, social unrest will prevent continued economic growth and weaken the ability of the Republic to withstand North Korea's aggression and propaganda. When the majority harbors strong resentment of an unfair system, radical ideology offers appeal and young idealists become easy prey to demagogues.

Of course, it is unrealistic and unreasonable to expect a completely equal distribution of benefits and sacrifices. My goal is to make sure that all people, including entrepreneurs, workers, and farmers, participate in varying degrees in the enjoyment of the fruits of development and that no individual, group, region, or generation is forced to carry an unfairly heavy burden for the benefit of others.

My program also attempts to ensure that sacrifices required for economic growth are equitably shared among present and future generations. In this regard, the Park–Chun growth strategy appears to have put the cart before the horse. Their policies have been geared toward maximizing the aggregate growth rate without regard to the associated benefits and costs. The fundamental objective of any development program should be to benefit *all* people, including present and future generations. Rapid (but not necessarily maximum) economic growth is a corollary dictated by development needs.

Korea's foreign debt at the beginning of 1984 was $41 billion, the fourth-largest sum owed by any country, very close to that of number three, Argentina ($42 billion). In per capita terms, each Korean is in debt to foreign banks by about $1,000, a figure more than half of the 1983 per capita GNP ($1,884)! This staggering foreign debt is evidence that Presidents Park and Chun attempted to placate the demands of present generations at the expense of future generations. An unpopular ruler is most likely to seek such a short-term gain despite its long-term peril. That is why Third World debt crises are invariably found in countries with undemocratic governments. The repeated warnings by many Korean leaders against excessive reliance on foreign debt would not have been ignored by a democratic government.

Price stability

In a monetary economy, in which transaction contracts are specified in terms of monetary units (as opposed to the commodity units of a barter economy), stability in price levels removes uncertainty and increases economic efficiency. Unfortunately, maintenance of price stability sometimes requires short-run sacrifices in growth. Thus, a careful balancing of the twin objectives of growth and price stability is needed.

The Park–Chun economic policy has sacrificed price stability in favor of rapid growth. Presidents Park and Chun have embarked on various projects that could not be financed by domestic savings and have relied on chronic deficit financing.[7] The annual rate of inflation between 1970 and 1981 averaged nearly 17 percent. President Park repeatedly proclaimed that he would balance the growth objective with appropriate consideration for price stability, but he never seriously carried out any anti-inflationary measure. Meanwhile, Taiwan, Singapore, and Hong Kong have shown that it is possible to achieve almost equally high long-term growth rates with price stability and better sectoral balances.

Another factor that prevented President Park from bringing about price stability was the constant need to bail out badly managed enterprises. Many of these had been created by Park's cronies, not to take advantage of perceived business opportunities but to receive government allocations of favors. They usually started new businesses with virtually no capital of their own. When the inevitable bankruptcies confronted them, they turned to the government for additional funds and the government proved to be very obliging. As a consequence, the monetary policy of Korea has been a shambles.

A democratic government is under pressure, except in wartime, to seek a proper balance between rapid growth and price stability. Furthermore, a democratic government cannot afford to support big business alone to the neglect of other interests, or it will not be permitted to stay in power very long. I believe it is necessary to make Korea's monetary authority independent (it is now under the control of the Ministry of Finance) in order to prevent future financial scandals and to ensure a monetary policy appropriate to the twin objectives of growth and stability.

An outline of my program

The basic approach of my program is set out in my 1971 book (published in Korean) and various interview articles, some of which were printed in English or in Japanese. I have also expressed some of my more recent thoughts in my *Letters from Prison*.[8] The present book, while maintaining the basic approach of the 1971 volume, will be recast in order to incorporate more comprehensively my recent thoughts and my observations on and evaluation of present Korean and world economic trends. The following is an outline of my program.

Reliance on the market

Some Western observers of Korean economic growth regard it as an example of the superiority of a free-market-oriented development program. Needless to say, the Korean economy relies more on the market than does a communist economy. However, it is not a free-market economy. In fact, the economy of Korea is very tightly controlled by the central government, which is active in almost every aspect of economic decision making, including pricing, investment allocation, credit rationing, and labor–management relations.[9]

Because these market interventions have often been politically motivated, they have produced inefficient allocations of resources that have stunted the growth of small or medium-sized enterprises, caused stagnation of the agricultural sector, and unilaterally imposed sacrifices on labor. These very costly mistakes have been masked by impressive aggregate growth rates. The spectacular growth rates of the past two decades were possible, despite the adverse actions of the government, because of Korea's great human assets. Korea's growth rates would have been even more impressive had the government refrained from such foolish intervention in the market. The guiding principle of my program will be to rely on the market mechanism.

A corollary of the principle of reliance on the market mechanism is to promote the competitive function of the market. Most important in this regard is removal of trade barriers. In this era of international economic interdependency, free trade is the best antitrust weapon. However, in certain cases in which competition via free trade is not feasible, appropriate measures, including enactment and enforcement of antitrust laws, must be applied. Unfortunately, under a noncommunist dictatorship such as that in Korea, monopolistic and oligopolistic businesses and the ruling class tend to collaborate.[10] Therefore, unnecessary trade barriers are selectively applied and antitrust laws selectively ignored in order to grant or preserve monopolistic market powers of a few entrepreneurs. The result of such a policy has been unfairly high prices paid by domestic consumers for poor-quality products.[11] A more competitive domestic market will benefit domestic consumers with lower prices and higher quality. In addition, competition at home will prevent dumping in foreign markets and thereby contribute to more harmonious relations with Korea's trading partners.

Also of importance in promoting competition is the balance of power between labor and management. In the United States, it has been recently recognized that the absence of harmony in labor–management relations is detrimental to productivity enhancement and thus competitiveness in the world market. Suddenly, America has discovered the cooperative spirit of Japanese labor–management relations and begun to adapt it to the American scene, despite the difficulty of making adjustments for the cultural differences.

To a great extent, Korea's Confucian tradition resembles Japan's. Historically, labor–management relations in Korea have been cooperative. Unfortunately, however, the Park–Chun policy of preserving international competitiveness by keeping wages low has led to open suppression of labor unions by violent means. The government's use of violence and arbitrary laws has left deep scars in the nation's labor–management relations. This is a very serious mistake that must be immediately corrected before it is too late. Given the Confucian tradition of making face-saving compromises and avoiding violence, I believe labor–management relations can be reasonably harmonious and cooperative, if the government avoids oppression of labor. Rather than oppressing one side, the government ought to be an impartial mediator and peacemaker.

The role of government: to promote market efficiency

The principle of relying on the market defines the role of government in my program. Government's role in the economic sphere is to ensure the proper functioning of markets and to promote competition when necessary. However, in some areas of market economy, even a perfectly competitive market fails to allocate resources efficiently and government action is called for to guide the market toward efficiency. For example, a competitive market does not provide incentives for firms to care for the environment. In this situation, the government can induce firms to reduce damage to the environment by imposing charges based on the extent of the damage. In general, where the market fails to ensure efficient allocation of resources, taxes and regulations can be used to create incentives for efficiency.

Another role of government in a market economy is to stabilize the economy by using monetary and fiscal tools of macroeconomic policy. Business cycles are unavoidable features of market-oriented economies. One important lesson learned by industrialized countries during the 1930s was that the economic consequences of government inaction during a recession could be disastrous. On the other hand, the experiences of the 1970s taught us another valuable lesson—that policy measures aimed at demand management are not appropriate for coping with supply shocks. Thus, the effectiveness of macroeconomic policy tools differs from situation to situation, and recognition of this limitation is essential in avoiding policies that do more harm than good. As the Korean economy grows, macroeconomic stabilization policy will become increasingly important.

Even with a government policy of promoting competition, monopolistic or monopsonistic areas—especially in certain labor markets—will continue to exist. In this case, the government has an important role to play in preventing monopolistic or monopsonistic exploitation of the market. Thus, if an employer can exercise monopsony power over workers, the government needs to protect the welfare of the workers. On the other hand, if a monopolistic labor union forces management into unreasonable and inflationary wage concessions, the government ought to persuade the union to be reasonable. Finally, in a situation where management and unions both have considerable market power, the government must act as an impartial arbitrator and prevent a costly standoff between the two parties.

The role of entrepreneurs: profit-making and social responsibilities

When a prominent Korean businessman contributes a large sum of money to a charitable cause, news media praise him for fulfilling his "social responsibility as an entrepreneur" or for his "entrepreneurial morality." Charity must be appreciated and praised, but we should not confuse an individual's personal morality with a businessman's social responsibility. In fact, the conspicuous generosity of Korean businessmen is often aimed at masking their immoral behavior in business activities. I believe an entrepreneur has several important social responsibilities in a free-market economy.

First, an entrepreneur must have faith in the free-market economic system and a sense of pride and mission in the development and defense of the system. He must promote the system through creativity and risk taking. It would be hypocritical for one to preach in favor of free market only when it suits him and then to ask for government intervention when market competition gets tough.

Second, an entrepreneur has the responsibility of supplying goods and services, within the parameters given in the market, of the highest quality at the lowest price. This is assured in a perfectly competitive market. However, in the real world, where markets are not perfectly competitive, it is the social obligation of an entrepreneur to work toward providing high quality at a low cost.

Third, he has an obligation to pay his employees fair and equitable wages that are commensurate with productivity gains, and to provide a wholesome and safe work environment.

Fourth, he must reinvest a portion of his profits, thus creating new job opportunities and helping to improve the overall standard of living of the nation.

Fifth, an entrepreneur must constantly seek to improve productivity. A complacent businessman jeopardizes not only his own business but also the welfare of his employees and the overall standard of living.

Sixth, if a firm monopolizes a market as a result of producing a better product at a lower price, it should not be held responsible for that result, although it should be responsible for what it does afterwards.[12] However, an entrepreneur should not be permitted to mobilize political power or monetary might in order to annex smaller firms and thereby monopolize the market.

Seventh, as a result of technological advancement and globalization of the market, enterprises are becoming ever larger and are no longer mere business firms. Rather, they have become social institutions with a social responsibility to contribute to the prosperity of the economy, to price stability, to the preservation and expansion of job opportunities, and to the maintenance of a clean environment.

Not all entrepreneurs will show responsibility in all these areas. It is the role of the government to nudge entrepreneurs toward living up to their responsibilities by promoting competition, by arbitrating labor–management relations, and by using various tax incentives and regulations. Of course, the government must be mindful of preserving market incentives in its attempts to encourage entrepreneurs toward "good behavior."

The role of labor unions: rights and responsibilities

Just as entrepreneurs have social responsibilities, so do labor unions. Needless to say, the primary obligation of the unions is to look after the interests of workers. Their social obligation is to seek fair and equitable wages and work rules and to avoid putting their own interests above those of the entire nation. Assuming that the present unfairness has been removed, this implies that their wage demands must reflect productivity gains.

Another important obligation of the unions is the promotion and preservation of a cooperative relationship with management. Of course, this implies that management should reciprocate in the same spirit. The importance of a cooperative labor–management relationship has been widely recognized throughout the world during the past decade. A cooperative relationship, by definition, requires moderation on *both* sides. The mistaken notion that labor can do no wrong can be detrimental to the economy.

While it is important to recognize the responsibilities of labor unions, the most urgent current priority in labor-relations policy is an institutional guarantee of the basic rights of workers. For over two decades, Korea's workers have borne most of the sacrifices required for growth. Such unilateral imposition of sacrifices on labor is not only unfair, but also a cause of social unrest. Furthermore, impoverishment of the workers has restricted the growth of domestic markets and thus led to excessive dependence on foreign markets, making the Korean economy vulnerable to fluctuations in the world economic conditions.[13]

Therefore, for the sake of social stability, cooperative labor–management relations, and domestic-market growth, the rights of workers must be vigorously upheld so that workers and employers both enjoy equal rights. Workers' rights should not be upheld as an act of mercy by any group or the government; rather, workers should be enabled to participate in production, management, and negotiation so that they can claim and protect their own rights.

NOTES

1. World Bank, *The World Development Report 1981* (New York: Oxford University Press, 1981), 134–35.
2. *New York Times*, 2 August 1983, A2.
3. William Loehr and John P. Powelson, *The Economics of Development and Distribution* (New York: Harcourt Brace Jovanovich, 1981), 8.
4. Kim, Dae Jung, *Kim Dae Jung tseeui Daejung Kyungje* (Seoul: Bum-woo Publishing Co., 1971). This book was developed from my unpublished M.A. thesis, "Mass-Participatory Economy," Kyung-Hee University, 1970.
5. For an insightful discussion of this problem, see Arthur M. Okun, *Equality and Efficiency: The Big Trade-off* (Washington, D.C.: Brookings Institution, 1975).
6. This aspect of Korea's economic development under Park and Chun is discussed further in Chapter 6.
7. The central government budget (calendar-year basis) has been in the red every year during the past two decades except 1979. See Bank of Korea, *Economic Statistics Yearbook* (1983), 5.
8. Kim Dae Jung, *Minjogue Hanul Anko* (New York: Galilee Moongo, 1983).
9. Some Western observers are now beginning to recognize this fact. For example, *The Wall Street Journal* (13 April 1984, 17) reports that "The economy is centrally directed: A government-drafted five-year plan charts the way for Korea's nine huge industrial conglomerates."
10. According to Mancur Olson, free trade mitigates the undesirable influence of the distributional coalitions (special-interest groups), which tends to accumulate over time in a stable democracy. See his *Rise and Decline of Nations* (New Haven: Yale University Press, 1982).
11. Empirical evidence for this proposition will be presented and discussed in Chapter 5.
12. I am indebted for this insight to Joseph A. Schumpeter, *Capitalism, Socialism and Democracy*, 3d ed. (New York: Harper & Brothers, 1950).
13. For further analysis of this aspect, see Chapter 4.

2

A brief review of Korea's post-war economy

A period of economic dislocations: 1945–1953

The Korean economy during Japanese colonial rule (1910–1945) was highly dependent on Japan for capital, management skills, and technology. The sudden break of the Korean–Japanese economic link and subsequent partition of Korea along the 38th parallel created serious economic dislocations. In particular, because industries, natural resources, and population were unevenly distributed, the partition had a devastating effect on the economy of South Korea.

At the time of partition, over 90 percent of Korea's power generation came from the North and, because of its abundant natural resources, most of the heavy industries were located there. Because of the lack of electric power supply, South Korea's industries were crippled by the partition, and had to operate far below their capacities (see Table 2-1). In addition to the

Table 2-1. Manufacturing output, 1940 and 1948
(million constant 1948 won)

	Manufacturing output in 1940		South Korea's manufacturing output, 1948
	All Korea	South Korea	
Metal	49.2	4.9	2.2
Machinery	19.3	13.9	3.4
Chemicals	181.5	30.7	15.2
Textiles	72.8	61.5	21.6
Foods	118.8	76.0	6.6
Ceramics	15.7	4.3	1.4
Printing	7.0	6.2	1.6
Handicrafts	7.6	4.9	0.7
Other	59.0	45.7	0.0
Total	530.9	248.1	52.6

Source: Bank of Korea, Economic Statistics Yearbook, 1949.

sharp decline in manufacturing output, South Korea was suffering from severe food shortages caused by a rapid growth of population as refugees migrated from North Korea and overseas Koreans, mostly from Japan, were repatriated. Shortages of commodities and a rapid expansion of the money supply caused hyperinflation; retail prices in Seoul were about 123 times higher in 1949 than in 1945.

Although industrial production was drastically reduced immediately following the liberation and partition, production levels rose fairly rapidly during the next four years. For example, electric power generation almost tripled by 1949 and the production of nails increased to more than eight times the 1946 level. Despite such rapid growth, industrial output in 1949 was far below the previous peak achieved during the colonial period. Although a lack of comprehensive data prevents an accurate comparison, various production indexes reported by the Bank of Korea indicate that the 1949 level of industrial output was no more than one-third of the 1940 level.[1]

Just when Korea's economy was being resuscitated, it was disrupted once again by the outbreak of war on 25 June 1950. Production levels during the first two years of the conflict dropped precipitously, and it was not until 1953, the year when the hostilities ceased, that output again reached 1949 levels. The recovery, however, was uneven; tungsten production for export, cigarettes and tobacco, paper and paper products, laundry soap, cement, and power generation recovered relatively quickly, but many other industries did not regain their 1949 levels until after the war.[2]

Post-Korean War reconstruction: 1953–1962

During the first four years following the armistice of July 1953, Korea's real GNP grew fairly rapidly. Even though a poor harvest resulting in a 6 percent decline in agricultural production slowed GNP growth in 1956 (0.4 percent), real GNP grew from 1953 to 1957 at an average annual rate of 4.7 percent (Table 2-2). Mining for export and light manufacturing for the domestic market grew rapidly during this period.

The rapid economic growth between 1953 and 1957 was fueled largely by foreign aid, which amounted to $1,294.4 million over that period (Table 2-2). Wartime hyperinflation, which had been as high as 530 percent (measured by the increase in the wholesale price index) during 1950–51, had been brought under control. Still, the rate of inflation, depending on the particular price index used, was averaging 36 to 37 percent per annum during the period 1953–57 (Table 2-2). Concern about inflation led to the application of a forceful anti-inflationary measure in 1957 and 1958. As a result, price levels were stabilized in 1958 and 1959, but at the cost of an economic slowdown. To make matters worse, President Rhee's increasingly inept, corrupt, and autocratic management of the economy and the resulting series of political upheavals, including the 1960 Student Revolution and the 1961 military coup, led to continued economic slowdown up to 1962. Although

Table 2-2. GNP growth, foreign aid, and price indexes

Year	Real GNP growth (%)	Foreign aid (million $)	Price indexes (1970 = 100)		
			GNP deflator	Wholesale	CPI[a]
1953	—	194.2	5.7	8.2	7.5
1954	5.5	153.9	7.5	10.5	10.2
1955	5.4	236.7	12.4	19.1	17.3
1956	0.4	326.7	16.2	25.1	21.2
1957	7.6	382.9	19.5	29.2	26.1
1958	5.5	321.3	19.4	27.3	25.3
1959	3.8	222.2	19.9	28.0	26.4
1960	1.1	245.4	21.8	31.0	28.6
1961	5.6	199.2	25.1	35.1	30.9
1962	2.2	239.3	28.6	38.4	32.9

Source: Bank of Korea, *Economic Statistics Yearbook*, various years.
a. Seoul consumer price index.

a 12 percent increase in agricultural output helped to shore up the overall growth rate in 1961, a subsequent decline of 6 percent in that sector lowered the GNP growth rate to 2.2 percent in 1962. The result was that, during the five-year period from 1957 to 1962, real GNP grew at an average annual rate of 3.6 percent, compared with 4.7 percent during the period 1953–57. The growth of per capita real GNP from 1957 to 1962 was meager because the population grew at an annual rate of 3.0 percent from 1955 to 1960.[3]

Assuming that manufacturing and mining output in 1953 was about one-third of the 1940 level, the 1940 output level was not recovered until 1963.[4] Thus, South Korea's economy stood still for nearly a quarter of a century, for various reasons. However, Korea's most important asset, human capital, rapidly increased during this period following the explosion of demand for education, which had been bottled up by the Japanese colonial government (Table 2-3). The foundation for the spectacular growth of the next two decades had been prepared following the liberation in 1945.

By 1960, as a result of this education fever, 94 percent of the primary-school-age group was enrolled in school.[5] Thus, virtually universal elementary education was achieved by the time General Park Chung Hee took over the government in 1961. Secondary and higher education enrollments also skyrocketed. This dramatic rise in the level of education was facilitated partly by government policy but mostly by a marriage of opportunities made available by enterprising (!) private educational institutions and a feverish desire for education rooted in Korean culture.

Table 2-3. Student enrollment trends (thousand persons)

Level	1945	1956	1960
Elementary school	1,366	2,921	3,621
Secondary school	84	748	792
Higher education	8	97	101

Source: *Education in Korea* (Seoul: National Institute of Education, 1977), 141–46.

Park Chung Hee's five-year plans and records

The 1961 military coup led by General Park marked the beginning of a new economic regime in which direct government action frequently superseded market functions and indirect interventions were applied by decrees and regulations. Nevertheless, the Park administration, from 1961 to 1979, saw spectacular growth in real GNP and exports (Table 2-4). As a result, Korea's per capita income, which had stood at the meager level of $80 in 1960, rose to $1,884 in 1983 (in current dollars).

Although the rapid growth in exports had started shortly after the end of the Korean War, it had begun from a very low base. The phenomenal continuing expansion of exports during the next two decades and the rise in the share of manufactured goods from about 15 percent to over 90 percent of total exports must thus be regarded as an unusual achievement by the Korean economy. The emphasis on exports was proper, given the limited size of the domestic market and the large pool of unemployed or under-employed people. However, chronic double-digit inflation proved to be a serious problem.

In 1962, the military government of Park Chung Hee introduced the first five-year economic development plan by modifying the National Reconstruction Plan of the Chang Myon administration (which Park had overthrown). Since then, Korea's development plans have been carried out in terms of a series of five-year plans. Actual GNP growth rates exceeded the plan targets during the first three five-year-plan periods (see Table 2-5). Although the realized annual growth rate of 5.5 percent during the fourth five-year-plan period was significantly lower than the target growth rate of 9.2 percent, primarily because of the 1980 recession, it was not a bad record by international standards.[6]

In terms of aggregate growth records, therefore, President Park's accomplishment looks impressive. However, his obsession with surpassing targets and his administration's excessive interference with market functions created many serious problems that, except for the constant inflationary pressure, are not very well recognized abroad.

Table 2-4. GNP growth, exports, and share of manufactured
exports and inflation (in 1975 constant prices)

Year	Real GNP growth (%)	Growth of exports (%)	Share of manufactured exports (%)	Inflation[a] (%)
1955	5.4	25.2	15.1	69.6
1956	0.4	−10.9	14.4	22.5
1957	7.6	35.7	21.0	23.1
1958	5.5	26.3	15.7	−3.1
1959	3.8	16.2	12.5	4.3
1960	1.1	19.7	14.2	8.3
1961	5.6	39.4	16.1	8.0
1962	2.2	12.6	19.3	6.5
1963	9.1	9.0	45.5	20.7
1964	9.6	23.5	49.0	29.5
1965	5.8	35.9	61.0	13.6
1966	12.7	42.4	61.4	11.2
1967	6.6	32.7	67.2	10.9
1968	11.3	39.5	74.3	10.8
1969	13.8	36.1	76.6	12.3
1970	7.6	19.6	77.4	15.9
1971	9.4	20.4	80.7	13.5
1972	5.8	36.9	84.0	11.7
1973	14.9	55.4	84.3	3.1
1974	8.0	−3.1	84.9	24.3
1975	7.1	16.6	81.6	25.3
1976	15.1	43.0	87.7	15.3
1977	10.3	25.7	84.9	10.1
1978	11.6	17.5	88.5	14.4
1979	6.4	−3.6	89.2	18.3
1980	−6.2	9.9	90.1	28.7
1981	6.2	17.4	90.6	21.3
1982	5.6	3.3	91.7	7.3
1983	9.5	15.7	—	2.2

Source: Bank of Korea, *Economic Statistics Yearbook*, various years, and *Dong-A Ilbo*, 21 March and 27 July 1984.

a. Seoul consumer price index up to 1965, CPI for all cities thereafter.

Table 2-5. Five-year development plan targets and results
(average annual rates)

Plan Period		Real GNP growth (%)	Unemployment rate (%)	GNP deflator change (%)	Export growth (%)
1962–66	Plan	7.1	14.8	n.a.	28.0
	Actual	7.8	7.1	19.3	38.6
1967–71	Plan	7.0	5.0	n.a.	17.1
	Actual	9.7	4.5	13.9	33.8
1972–76	Plan	8.6	4.0	n.a.	22.7
	Actual	10.1	3.9	21.0	32.7
1977–81	Plan	9.2	3.8	8.8	16.0
	Actual	5.5	4.5	19.9	10.5
1982–86	Plan	7.6	4.0	9.5	11.4

Source: Economic Planning Board (as reported in *Dong-A Ilbo*, 14 July 1983); Bank of Korea, *Economic Statistics Yearbook*, various years.

Recent crises

The economic situation of Korea in 1978 was, according to the Park government, the "greatest boom since Tan-Kun" (mythical founder-king of the Korean nation who, according to the myth, descended from heaven to benefit the people and founded the ancient Kingdom of Chosen in 2333 B.C.). Park also proclaimed that in the 1970s the Korean economy would achieve a highly developed stage in which lack of demand would be a problem and, therefore, consumption an economic virtue. In reality, 1978 marked the end of prolonged economic expansion and was followed by an economic slowdown in 1979, the year when Park was assassinated, and a decline of real GNP in 1980 for the first time since 1953, when GNP was first estimated.

The economic slowdown, coupled with accelerating inflation (Table 2-4), ever-worsening dictatorial practices, and anti-labor policies, caused widespread discontent, which culminated in popular rebellion and the assassination of President Park in 1979. The ensuing political unrest and the effect of the 1979 OPEC price increase brought about the first recession in the post-Korean War history of the Republic. The administration of General Chun Doo Hwan, who shot his way into the presidency, has been plagued by a series of financial scandals, some of which have involved President

Chun's relatives. As a result, the financial market has been repeatedly disrupted and has had to be bailed out several times by massive infusions of
money from the central bank.

At present, Korea's economy is well on its way to expansion, regis-
tering a 9.5 percent growth of real GNP in 1983. Such impressive growth
may continue for a while, but it will be only a temporary phenomenon.
Korea's income inequality and market concentration are becoming worse
each year, and inflationary pressure is building again. The resulting discontent of the people with economic injustice, in combination with their
dissatisfaction with political oppression, is causing political instability, which
in turn is threatening to thwart economic development. Moreover, in an era
of high technology, the government's preoccupation with suppressing student demonstrations has prevented adequate investment in education and
research and development. For these reasons, Korea will be unable to continue the rapid economic growth of the past two decades unless there is a
fundamental change in economic policy and democratization of the political
process.

Factors responsible for the rapid growth

Real GNP grew fairly quickly immediately following the end of the
Korean War. However, annual growth rates averaging nearly 10 percent
did not occur before the second half of the 1960s. It is thus only natural to
hypothesize that President Park, who ruled Korea with an iron fist from
1961 to 1979, was somehow responsible for the spectacular growth of Korea's
economy. Park did instill confidence in the nation's ability to make improvements and, by placing economic development high on the priority list,
motivated both the people and bureaucrats. Concrete policy measures, such
as the exchange-rate reforms of 1964 and 1965 and the interest-rate reform
of 1965, also contributed to economic growth. However, many wise policy
actions were frequently undone by subsequent policy reversals, and increasingly corrupt and autocratic practices undermined the efficient allocation of resources. On balance, I would consider President Park's economic
policy severely flawed because it led to polarization of the nation by region,
by income class, and by economic sector.

It is often argued that Park deserves credit for Korea's rapid economic
growth because his strong government provided political stability. In fact,
the political situation under President Park was more like a temporary balance on a razor's edge accompanied by a constant fear of falling off the edge.
On the surface, his tight-fisted rule made it possible to maintain stability
for a while. But, as he became increasingly autocratic, the political situation
became increasingly unstable. His assassination in 1979 and the ensuing
political turmoil is evidence that he was responsible for political instability
rather than stability.

Over the past two decades the world's fastest-growing economies have been Asian countries that share a similar Confucian tradition—Korea, Taiwan, Hong Kong, and Singapore. At the same time, another country with a similar cultural background, Japan, has risen to the top echelon of world economic powers. These Asian countries have in common, among other things, a very high regard for education. As noted earlier, Korea's work force was fairly well educated and ready to realize its productive potential by the beginning of the 1960s. Of course, the fact that world trade expanded rapidly during the 1960s and the 1970s helped a great deal. But the same world economic environment did not benefit all developing countries evenly. Some countries managed to grow faster than others. Why?

Many countries blessed with abundant natural resources remain stagnant because of a lack of human resources necessary to take full advantage of their other endowments. A few countries are blessed with abundant natural resources *and* human resources. These are the leading economic powers in the world. A third group of countries, which lack natural resources but have well-educated people, have shown that they can overcome the natural-resource handicap. The Asian NICs (newly industrializing countries) belong to this third group. Moreover, Japan has demonstrated that, despite a natural-resource handicap, it can effectively compete with those blessed with abundant human and natural resources. An economy is a system of production, exchange, and distribution that is managed by people. I believe, therefore, that a people's management capability is the most decisive factor. Of course, abundant natural resources help a great deal, as demonstrated by the wealth of some of the OPEC nations. But natural resources are finite, and in the end human resources determine the economic power of a nation.

Should President Park be given credit for harnessing the nation's human resources? Even as a political rival of Mr. Park, I must admit that fairly impressive economic *growth* was achieved under his government. In addition, he instilled in the Korean people a positive attitude of "we can do it," and recognized the importance of foreign markets. However, these accomplishments cannot mask his failures.

The fact that Korea is one of the world's largest debtors indicates that Park's economic policy was not very prudent. Moreover, most of the foreign debt has been wasted on uneconomical projects. For example, near the end of the 1960s the Park administration was forced to take drastic measures to save insolvent enterprises that had been financed by foreign debt under government loan guarantees. The government had to admit that nearly 80 percent of the foreign-debt-financed enterprises under government loan guarantees were insolvent. The insolvent enterprises were taken over and managed by banks and subsequently handed over to large conglomerates.

These foreign-debt-financed projects had been conceived by bureaucrats, and government loan guarantees were approved on the basis of political connections rather than economic feasibility. Thus, it was inevitable that the Korean government would face the same problem repeatedly. President Park had an ambition to build heavy and chemical industries. During the

1970s he made a major effort to build these industries, relying heavily on foreign capital. Many of these projects were pushed through even though Korea did not have the necessary technology and management capability. Moreover, because of inadequate market research, most of these industries were operating substantially below capacity (some at the 20 to 30 percent level) and eventually became insolvent. Once again, the government had to take drastic measures to save them. The rescue operation for these industries, which started toward the end of the Park administration, continues to this day. Most recently, Korea's construction industry has been added to the list of those that are being bailed out by the government and commercial banks.[7]

Such wasteful use of precious foreign capital has not only left the Korean people with a crushing debt burden, but also endangered the nation's banking institutions. Furthermore, in the process of creating foreign-debt-financed white elephants, many businessmen made fortunes by diverting funds. Thus, the Korean people say, "When enterprises go bankrupt, their owners get richer." In a nutshell, Park's economic policy, which his successor Chun has vowed to follow zealously, was responsible for the extreme imbalance among the three objectives of growth, equality, and price stability. Furthermore, Park was responsible for large-scale corruption, enriching himself and his cronies at the expense of national welfare. This is why rapid economic growth has been accompanied by acute polarization, social unrest, and political unrest. In comparison with these problems created by President Park, his contributions are very limited. If Korea, with such well-educated and disciplined human resources, had been under a democratic government like that of West Germany or Japan, it would have achieved a much better economic *development* on a more robust and promising foundation.

NOTES

1. Bank of Korea, *Annual Economic Review*, 1955.
2. *Ibid.*
3. Bank of Korea, *Economic Statistics Yearbook*, 1983.
4. See Charles R. Frank, Kwang Suk Kim, and Larry Westphal, *Foreign Trade Regimes and Economic Development: South Korea* (New York: National Bureau of Economic Research, 1975), 9. (Growth rates for this sector are not available for years before 1953.)
5. World Bank, *World Development Report 1981* (New York: Oxford University Press, 1981).
6. For the period 1970–79, growth in real GNP for the middle-income developing countries averaged 5.5 percent per annum. See World Bank, *op. cit.*, 136.
7. *Wall Street Journal*, 31 August 1984.

3

Politics and economics under the Park and Chun regimes

Those who give President Park credit for Korea's spectacular economic growth during the 1960s and 1970s believe that his strong government was instrumental in providing political stability, which is considered to be a necessary condition for economic development. These observers are typically unaware of the political instability created by Park's authoritarian rule and are too impressed by Korea's aggregate growth records to see anything negative about his economic policies. However, it is too simplistic to conclude that Park Chung Hee was responsible for the rapid economic growth simply because it occurred during his tenure.

Although President Park did make some contribution to the economic development of Korea by encouraging a positive attitude and aggressive search for markets, his economic policies included many ill-conceived measures that were detrimental to the national goal of developing a well-balanced economy. Most of these ill-conceived policies were the inevitable results of dictatorship, which allowed no criticism of his policies and no mechanism for checks and balances. Some important examples are discussed below.

Get-rich-quick attitude

When the military junta took over the government in 1961, it had to pledge to restore civilian rule soon in order to placate the popular yearning for democracy. After all, a dictator (President Rhee) had been overthrown by the people only a year before General Park deposed the elected government of Prime Minister Chang. To perpetuate his rule in civilian disguise, Park and his party needed a huge political fund. His military government made many scandalous business deals, in which favored businessmen received special licenses to import restricted and highly demanded commodities or permits to purchase government properties at give-away prices. In exchange for these favors, businessmen had to give huge kick-backs to Park's party, but still the deals were enormously profitable. Out of these deals were created many giant conglomerates. Thus, the smartest thing for businessmen to do was to look for contacts with high-ranking officials rather than to look for investment opportunities. Such attitudes remain pervasive to this day.

Sometimes bribes are forcefully demanded of business firms. In a country where the government is almighty, falling into its disfavor is virtually the kiss of death, as evidenced by the sudden bankruptcies of large corporations such as the Yul San Corporation.[1] Americans learned about the seriousness of this problem when a Congressional hearing following the so-called Koreagate scandal revealed that American oil companies and Japanese concerns had been forced to make multimillion dollar political contributions to Park Chung Hee to finance his presidential election campaign in 1971. To this day, businessmen in Korea are constantly pressured by government agents to make political contributions. Of course, the government has to keep the geese alive so that they will continue to lay golden eggs. Thus, those who cooperate with the government are well rewarded with profits from their monopolistic holds on the market, low-interest loans, government contracts at inflated prices, and so on.

Most new business opportunities have been discovered by small or medium-sized firms, which do not enjoy these special government favors. Whenever smaller firms make profitable investments, however, large corporations gobble them up immediately. Because of ubiquitous government intervention in all markets, nearly all financial resources are monopolized by the large firms, which thus have no difficulty in financing these takeovers.[2] As a result, big businesses in Korea are getting bigger by leaps and bounds.

The result is a very wasteful allocation of resources, including entrepreneurial talents. The only consolation is that, as giant conglomerates gobble up smaller profitable firms, at least some part of the nation's resources is used efficiently. The resulting concentration of the market power, however, is not acceptable. As long as the domestic market is open to imports, such concentration would not seriously impair the competitiveness of the market. However, these conglomerates can count on the government to protect their markets. The concentration of market power and income will be discussed in Chapter 5.

Anti-labor policy

In a modern economy in which hired workers constitute the majority or a sizable minority, organized labor can be a powerful political force. Therefore, no dictator can tolerate independent labor unions. The working class must be forbidden to organize or forced to belong to government-controlled unions. Whether in a communist dictatorship or in a right-wing dictatorship, allowing workers the freedom to organize independent unions and engage in collective actions is tantamount to nurturing a powerful opposition force. Thus, Presidents Park and Chun could not tolerate labor movements in Korea any more than General Jaruzelski could tolerate the Solidarity movement in Poland.

Justification for anti-labor policies may vary from country to country. In Korea under Park Chung Hee and Chun Doo Hwan, it was argued that a "low-wage" policy was needed to preserve the international competitiveness of Korean products. Those who engaged in union activities not sanctioned by the government were subjected to brutal violence and imprisonment. The economic consequences of this anti-labor policy will be discussed in Chapter 6.

Too many government enterprises

To reward the generals and colonels who have supported military dictatorship and to ensure the continuing support of the armed forces, Presidents Park and Chun have appointed a large number of retired military officers as executives of various government and quasi-government enterprises. To make room for these appointments, the Park and Chun regimes have created many new public enterprises and have also replaced many career executives with retired military officers. The economic consequence of such a strategy has been, to say the least, very wasteful.

First, the creation of government and quasi-government enterprises has hindered development of private enterprises. Since these public enterprises lack profit motivation, it is inevitable that their managements would be inefficient. For example, the government attempts to smooth out seasonal fluctuations in grain prices, but enterprising private grain dealers could perform this function more efficiently and farmers would be better served.[3] Instead, government agencies lord it over the Korean farmers.

Second, the incompetence of management teams appointed because of their loyalty to Park or Chun, rather than their management skills, has proven a very serious problem.[4] In 1983, Dow Chemical Company, which had made the largest American investment in Korea, withdrew from Korea, citing this very problem as its main reason for the withdrawal. A Dow executive said that the American management team had not been able to work well with the Korean former generals, who had no experience and ability in managing business firms, and he publicly warned other would-be American investors to stay out of Korea. The inefficient management of these public enterprises not only wastes taxpayers' money but scares away potential foreign investors.[5]

Finally, these public enterprises, which have been created as a high-class welfare program for the retired generals and colonels, have become hotbeds of large-scale corruption. They award contracts only to big businesses with clout and the ability to bribe, while smaller firms are shut out. These contracts are usually overpriced, in collusion with contractors, and the excess payments are then returned as bribes to the executives. Private management of these enterprises will not only reduce corruption but increase the nation's economic efficiency by improving the quality of management and by allowing competition among private firms instead of government monopoly.[6]

Regional discrimination

Among the many ill-advised practices of President Park Chung Hee, the most dangerous was his consistent bias in favor of his home region. In particular, Park practiced extreme regional discrimination in appointments and promotions of military officers and civil servants. Moreover, his home region received the highest priority in industrial-location decisions while other regions were systematically ignored.

The result is a very uneven regional economic balance and inefficient use of human resources. Worst of all, this practice of regional discrimination has seriously undermined national unity. When divisiveness runs to the extreme, economic gains can be quickly reversed and the preservation of a republic becomes nearly impossible, as is seen in Northern Ireland and Lebanon. Fortunately, Korea is not yet in such a state, despite twenty years of regional discrimination. But the Republic will eventually disintegrate if such divisive policies continue in the future. For this reason, the regional discrimination practiced by Park Chung Hee and Chun Doo Hwan must be regarded as the most serious offense to the national welfare.

The education problem

Korea's greatest asset is its human resources. Fortunately, Korean parents have always been very willing to sacrifice financially, frequently selling off properties and borrowing heavily, in order to educate their children. In this sense, Korean parents are largely responsible for the miraculous economic growth achieved despite the stifling presence of a totalitarian government. The dictatorial governments of Park and Chun, however, have proved to be the most difficult obstacle on the road to high-quality higher education in Korea.

The absence of academic freedom in Korea has prevented quality improvement in education, and this has been a major cause of student discontent. In addition, democratic demands of the people have frequently been advanced by university students, who were inspired and supported by some professors. These students and professors have thus been constantly in conflict with the government. Universities have been repeatedly shut down by the government, and student activists and courageous professors have been jailed and expelled. Professors who manage to avoid the wrath of the government by failing to speak out on social injustice do not enjoy the respect of their students. As a result, higher education has been constantly disrupted, and the universities are operating with a severe shortage of qualified and respected professors.

Until now, Korea has been able to adopt advanced technologies from the industrialized countries, but as international competition gets tougher, Korea must rely increasingly on itself in developing new technologies that will be competitive with those of the industrialized countries. Unless a peaceful and free learning environment is restored soon, the Korean economy will pay dearly for its lost educational opportunities. Of course, the government always holds the students and the professors responsible for the disruptions, but that amounts to blaming the victims.

Political stability, freedom, and economic development

No one disputes the proposition that political stability is a necessary condition for economic development. However, the misleading argument that dictatorship provides political stability must be rejected, for political stability is not achieved by the longevity of a regime but the durability of a political system. Dictatorship invites political instability, as evidenced by the constant clashes between government and religious leaders, opposition politicians, and students. The seeming stability under dictatorship is like being on a razor's edge. The political system in such a situation is constantly threatened with being pushed off the edge and thrown into chaos.

History demonstrates that, without freedom, economic development has its limit. For example, several European countries that were making progress in the early part of this century are now stagnant under communist dictatorships. On the other hand, the miraculous economic development of West Germany and Japan was achieved after these countries adopted democracy and allowed individual freedom. It cannot be a mere coincidence that, with the exception of a few oil-rich nations, the world's richest countries are all democratic countries. Although it is possible to achieve rapid economic growth up to a certain level under a dictatorial government, as is evidenced in Korea, Taiwan, and Brazil, we must ask, "For whom do we want fast growth?" If such growth is accompanied by the suppression of individual rights, it cannot be a sound economic development, and such a policy mix must be rejected. Why should any nation choose "growth with oppression" when "growth with freedom" is obtainable and longer-lasting?

NOTES

1. Yul San was one of the fastest-growing Korean corporations in the 1970s, but it was driven to bankruptcy in 1979 by the Park administration because the president disliked the firm's owner.
2. In 1982, through a prearranged bidding process, government-owned commercial banks were sold to a few conglomerates that were already in control of vast networks of manufacturing, distribution and retail outlets, and services.
3. For further discussion of this issue, see Chapter 7.
4. For a detailed report on this problem, see *Wall Street Journal*, 31 May 1984.
5. Partly for this reason, Korea has relied more on foreign debts than foreign direct in-

vestment. The resulting debt burden is seriously threatening a robust economic development. For further discussion of this issue, see Chapter 4.

6. For example, Korea Electric Power Company, which had been rated in early 1984 by government analysts as the best-managed government enterprise, was subsequently discovered to have overpaid power-plant construction expenses to Bechtel Corporation (u.s.) by tens of millions of dollars (*New York Times*, 4 July 1984). Considering that Bechtel had been implicated in bribe-giving to the Korean officials earlier that year, it is doubtful that such a large-scale overpayment was caused by an honest mistake, and it is clear that private enterprise would not have tolerated it.

4

Trade, foreign capital, and economic development

Foreign trade and economic development

There is no doubt that the phenomenal growth of exports contributed significantly to the economic growth of Korea. Export expansion increases a country's market size, making it possible to expand employment at home while reducing the cost of production through economies of scale. Furthermore, competition in the world market forces the export sector to greater efficiency over time, while the introduction of advanced technologies from abroad helps a developing country catch up with the developed countries. This line of reasoning contradicts the views of some radical economists, who tend to emphasize the shortcomings of an export-promoting development strategy.

According to the trade-pessimists, international trade between developed and developing countries tends to have adverse effects on the economies of developing countries due to (1) alleged secular deterioration of the terms of trade, (2) alleged instability of the export prices of primary products, which usually are the major export items of the developing countries, and (3) alleged dependency of the peripheries (developing countries) on the metropolis (developed countries) as an inevitable result of neocolonialism. It is my understanding that the first allegation has not been empirically validated. The second allegation is an arguable proposition but, as far as Korea is concerned, it has become irrelevant because primary products now account for less than 10 percent of total exports. The instability of export prices could be a negative factor so long as a developing country continues to rely on a small number of primary products for its export earnings. However, export promotion is a vehicle for developing diversified export industries, and therefore this strategy must be viewed positively, particularly if the prices of primary products are unstable.

The third allegation has been gaining popularity with the younger generation in Korea, mainly because of their disillusionment with the irresponsible policies of Park Chung Hee and Chun Doo Hwan, which have left the Korean economy dominated by foreign corporations and burdened by the world's fourth-highest foreign debt. Their disillusionment is quite understandable, but to embrace dependency theory is not very helpful.

The economic relationships between any two parties are not, in general, perfectly equitable, because their bargaining positions are not equal. This is a fact of life. Furthermore, there is nothing inherently bad about economic interdependence. But it *is* bad if the result of interdependence is a consistently unequal relationship. A developing country relying on exports to developed countries is, in principle, not much different from a small company supplying parts to a large manufacturer. In both cases, there is some element of dependency, and again that is a fact of life. The best thing a developing country can do to avoid unfair dependency is to develop itself! It is naive to think that a resource-poor developing country could develop itself in isolation from developed countries. Such naivete comes from a lack of understanding of market functions.

According to the dependency theory, because of the exploitive nature of the metropolis–periphery trade relationship, an underdeveloped country cannot catch up with developed countries by following the traditional trade-oriented development strategy. However, previously underdeveloped countries, notably Japan, have been fully successful and the Asian NICs partially successful in catching up with the developed countries using the traditional development strategy. Some of the propositions of dependency theory are not entirely baseless. However, the trouble with this theory is that it blames the developed countries for everything that goes wrong in the developing countries. There has been plenty of wrong-doing on the part of the developing countries, including Korea, which has benefited foreign corporations at the expense of the developing countries' people.[1]

Foreign trade in Korea

The most outstanding feature of Korea's economic development process during the 1960s and 1970s was the phenomenal growth of exports. Korea's export growth averaged 34.1 percent per year in real terms between 1960 and 1970 and 25.7 percent per year from 1970 to 1979.[2] No other country in the world was able to maintain an average annual export growth rate of over 20 percent for both decades.

Exceptionally rapid and steady growth occurred between 1961 and 1973 (Table 2-4) in response to the reforms of the exchange-rate system, various export incentives, and an aggressive search for export markets. The first in a series of reforms of the exchange-rate system was initiated by the Chang Myon administration, which attempted to unify the exchange-rate system and devalued the won by 100 percent in two months (January and February 1961). The unification of the exchange-rate system was completed by June 1961, a month after the coup d'etat, and was followed by further reforms in 1964 and 1965.

Korea's exports declined in 1974 for the first time in almost two decades and again in 1979, as a result of the worldwide trade contractions following the OPEC oil price increases. While the growth of exports between 1974 and 1979 was still very impressive, it was significantly slower than in the previous ten years. An important reason for the slowdown was that the exchange rate was pegged at 484 won to the dollar for over six years until 1980, when it averaged 659.9 won to the dollar. During this period, the Korean consumer price index was increasing, on the average, by 18.5 percent per year, compared with 8.9 percent for the United States, and so the pegging of the exchange rate resulted in an overvalued won.[3] Devaluations were necessary, but they were resisted because of their adverse effect on foreign-debt servicing. The overvaluation of the won had other serious repercussions in addition to encouraging imports and retarding the growth of exports. For example, the relative decline in the price of imported capital goods (compared with their social costs) resulted in excessive capital intensity at the expense of employment expansion.

As mentioned earlier, Korea's export expansion has not been accompanied by adequate development of the domestic market. As a result, exports have accounted for an excessively large share of GNP (see Table 4-1). The failure to nurture the industries supplying the domestic markets has also meant that the export sector has had to rely on imports for its inputs. Thus, the trade balance has always remained negative despite the extraordinary growth of exports. The major reason why the industries supplying domestic markets have failed to grow commensurately with the growth in exports has been the government's bias in tax and credit policies (to be discussed in Chapter 7). The consequences of this failure are illustrated by the fact that Korea's shipbuilding industry, which ranks number two in the world (behind Japan), has been relying on imported tools.

Excessive reliance on exports for growth and imports for inputs makes an economy vulnerable to external shocks, such as a sudden decrease in world demand or world supply. Expanding foreign trade is beneficial to the

**Table 4-1. Korea's trade dependency
(percent of GNP)**

Year	Exports	Imports	Total
1962	5.1	16.6	21.7
1965	8.5	15.9	24.4
1970	14.2	24.0	38.2
1975	28.1	36.9	65.0
1980	37.7	44.8	82.6
1982	40.3	41.2	81.5

Source: Bank of Korea, *Economic Statistics
Yearbook*, various issues.

Table 4-2. International comparison of
trade dependency ratios
(percent of GNP in 1981)

Country	Exports	Imports	Total
China	9.2	8.6	17.8
Hong Kong	106.5	112.4	218.9
Singapore	215.1	221.7	436.8
Korea	41.4	45.6	87.0
Japan	15.5	14.6	30.1
West Germany	29.6	28.7	58.2
France	21.8	25.0	46.8
United Kingdom	27.5	24.6	52.1
United States	9.4	10.4	19.8

Source: World Bank, *World Tables*, 3d ed., vol. 1
(Baltimore: Johns Hopkins University Press,
1983).

participating economies, but that does not mean that the domestic market
can be ignored. Expansion of the foreign and domestic markets ought to
occur simultaneously in order to maximize the benefits of trade-oriented
economic development. Of course, some countries are forced to rely more
on foreign trade because of their lack of natural resources or their small
populations, while others are more or less self-sufficient.

Is Korea excessively dependent on foreign trade? As Table 4-2 shows,
Korea was more heavily dependent on foreign trade than other selected
countries (except the two city-states, Hong Kong and Singapore). Even
Japan, the world's most successful exporter, had trade dependency ratios
about one-third those of Korea.

Since the size of the domestic market is constrained by the size of
population, a simple comparison of trade dependency ratios can be misleading. Trade dependency ratios must be compared with population sizes
as well. Table 4-3 compares trade dependency ratios and populations for
all countries whose per capita GNP in 1981 exceeded that of Korea and whose
total trade volume exceeded 80 percent of GDP. Among those with a total
trade dependency ratio above 80 percent of GDP, Korea has the largest
population. No other country has a population even half as large as Korea's.
Thus, it appears fair to say that Korea has the potential for developing its
domestic market and thereby reducing its excessive dependence on trade.
The causes of the failure to develop the domestic market and some remedial
policy proposals will be discussed in Chapter 7.

Table 4-3. Trade dependency ratios and populations of
selected countries[a] (ratios in percent of
GDP; population in thousands)

Country	Exports	Imports	Population
Korea	39.9%	44.0%	38,880
Hong Kong	109.2	115.3	5,154
Fiji	42.6	56.6	646
Malaysia	52.9	59.2	14,200
Singapore	113.2	213.9	2,444
Barbados	74.7	74.1	149
Panama	40.1	46.2	1,877
Suriname	40.6	62.9	353
Cyprus	51.4	65.7	623
Israel	43.2	58.4	3,954
Malta	81.5	89.9	364
Kuwait	70.6	41.2	1,464
Libyan Arab Republic	57.0	43.7	3,085
Saudi Arabia	70.3	30.8	9,305
Austria	42.2	42.8	7,554
Belgium	64.8	68.8	9,861
Iceland	41.4	42.3	231
Ireland	63.2	77.0	3,440
Luxembourg	79.4	84.4	364
Netherlands	58.3	54.6	14,246
Norway	47.8	39.8	4,100

Source: World Bank, World Tables, 3d ed., vols. 1 and 2, 1983.
a. Countries with higher per capita GNP than Korea and total
trade volume over 80 percent of GDP in 1981.

Foreign capital and economic development

The alarming growth in Korea's foreign debt, which reached $41 bil-
lion at the beginning of 1984, is not a recent phenomenon.[4] It started in the
middle of the 1960s, and by the end of President Park's rule in 1979, total
foreign debt had risen to $20.5 billion, or 34.1 percent of GNP. The debt
has continued to swell under the reign of Chun Doo Hwan, doubling its
size in just four years. The burden of foreign debt was such that, during

1983, the amount spent for foreign-debt servicing ($6.1 billion) exceeded the total new borrowing of $5.5 billion.⁵ New debt is now being used to repay old debt rather than to finance new investment projects.

Some people have been questioning the wisdom of using foreign debt for economic development, but this is an overreaction. Excessive or wasteful use of foreign debt is bad, but using foreign debt is not inherently bad. Under Park Chung Hee and Chun Doo Hwan, Korea's reliance on foreign debt has been excessive and very wasteful too, because of widespread corruption and unwise uses of debt in these administrations.

One fundamental reason for Korea's excessive reliance on foreign debt has been the inadequacy of domestic savings. For various reasons, Korea's personal saving rate (percent of disposable personal income not consumed) has been significantly lower than in other competing countries. Korea's average saving rate for the 1970s, 9.3 percent, was significantly higher than the average of less than 4 percent for the 1960s, but much too low for a developing country. For the period 1975–79, which included three of the highest recorded saving rates, the average was only 11.3 percent, significantly lower than the rates in many developed countries with fewer pressing needs for investment (see Table 4-4).

Faced with a low personal saving rate, the Park administration chose to supplement it with government financing and foreign debt. To some extent, such action was needed initially. However, a concerted effort to raise the personal saving rate was also needed, and this he failed to undertake. Savings were discouraged by the artificially low interest rates in the face of high inflation rates, and by uncertainty arising from political instability. To

Table 4-4. Personal saving rates, 1975–79

Country	Average saving rate
Korea	11.3%
Italy	23.1
Japan	21.5
France	17.2
West Germany	14.5
United Kingdom	12.2
Canada	10.3
Sweden	9.1
United States	6.3

Source: Bank of Korea, *Economic Statistics Yearbook*,
       1983; N.Y. Stock Exchange, *U.S. Economic
       Performance in a Global Perspective* (New York,
       1981), 27.

Table 4-5. Comparison of national saving
rates (percent of GNP)

Country	1960	1965	1970	1981
Korea	2.3	8.6	17.5	20.4
Hong Kong	8.4	23.0	25.8	25.5
Malaysia	24.0	20.4	22.8	23.9
Philippines	15.0	20.4	19.5	24.1
Singapore	−0.8	11.8	19.1	36.3
Canada	20.5	24.1	22.4	24.0
West Germany	29.8	28.5	29.9	23.7
Japan	33.1	33.2	40.2	32.0
United Kingdom	17.8	19.7	20.9	20.4
United States	19.8	21.4	18.6	19.4

Source: World Bank, *World Tables*, 3d ed., vol. 1, 1983.

make matters worse, Park Chung Hee and Chun Doo Hwan have often exaggerated a likelihood of invasion by North Korea in order to justify their oppressive rule.[6] As a result of their failure to raise the personal saving rate, Korea's national saving rate (including public saving) still remained well below those of Asian competitors and many developed countries (see Table 4-5).

To make up for the shortfall in the national saving rate, the Park and Chun regimes borrowed heavily from abroad. As a result, gross domestic investment averaged 29.4 percent of GDP during the period 1970–81, which was still lower than Japan's 33.3 percent but higher than Hong Kong's 26.7 percent.[7] These foreign savings undoubtedly contributed to economic growth, but the growth was achieved at the expense of the welfare of future generations. As argued before, maximizing the rate of growth is not necessarily the best development strategy. Because the debt burden became excessive, and new debt is now being used to repay the old, Korea will not be able to rely on foreign debt to finance new investment projects.

Instead of borrowing heavily from abroad, the Park and Chun regimes could have relied more on foreign direct investment as a means of supplementing the insufficient domestic saving. As shown in Table 4-6, Korea has made very little use of foreign direct investment, which accounted for only 5.7 percent of the total uses of foreign capital up to 1981. This is in sharp contrast with the more successful Asian competitors such as Singapore (85.1 percent) and Taiwan (64.2 percent).

As discussed earlier, part of the reason for the lack of foreign direct investment in Korea is the foreign investors' dislike of the Korean govern-

Table 4-6. Composition of foreign capital for selected countries, 1981
(cumulative amount, million U.S. dollars)

Source	Korea	Singapore	Taiwan	Brazil
Loans	19,964 (94.3%)	1,318 (14.9%)	1,739 (35.8%)	43,999 (71.6%)
Foreign direct investment	1,206 (5.7%)	7,520 (85.1%)	3,114 (64.2%)	17,480 (28.4%)

Source: World Bank, World Debt Tables, 1982–83; Republic of China, Taiwan Statistical Data Book, 1982; Economic Planning Board (Korea), Major Economic Indicators, 1982.

ment's practice of appointing ex-generals as executives. Another reason is the government's demand for exorbitant bribes as a condition for allowing foreign businesses in Korea. Privatization of government enterprises under a democratic government, which cannot interfere with private management decisions, will make Korea more attractive to foreign investors and thus help to reduce Korea's excessive reliance on foreign debt.

According to one study, the average annual growth of Korea's real GNP during the 1960s—nearly 10 percent—would have been reduced to about 6 percent had no foreign capital been used.[8] Since the average growth rate and the proportion of foreign savings in domestic capital formation during the 1970s were about the same as in the 1960s, the above estimate can be applied to the 1970s as an approximation. Thus, if Korea had halved its reliance on foreign debt, its growth rate would have averaged about 8 percent per year, even if one does not consider the possibility of more efficient use of foreign debt. I think an 8 percent growth rate is still pretty impressive, even for a developing country. Moreover, if Korea had relied more on foreign direct investment instead of foreign debt, an annual growth rate of nearly 10 percent could have been enjoyed with much lighter debt burden.

In sum, the use of foreign savings can be beneficial to economic development if it is done with caution and efficient allocation. Similarly, foreign direct investment can be beneficial to economic development, provided that the host government is free of corruption and lets the investors operate under rules that are fair and equitable to both the investors and the host nation. However, given the current crushing debt burden, Korea has no alternative but to curtail its use of foreign debt, make a concerted effort to raise the domestic saving rate, and encourage foreign direct investment. This will not be easy. Korea's political instability discourages personal saving, and the practice of converting ex-generals into executives of the government or quasi-government enterprises, coupled with political instability, is not conducive to attracting foreign direct investment.[9] Unless Korea recovers a genuine political stability under a democratic government, it will be forced to continue in the vicious cycle of borrowing from abroad to service foreign debt and thus accumulating more foreign debt.[10]

Free trade, foreign direct investment, and the world's future

Economists have long preached the benefits of free trade, but the task of persuading governments to practice it has proved to be formidable. The benefits of free trade are too abstract for an average citizen to comprehend fully, especially if he is in danger of losing his job because of foreign competition. Underdeveloped countries have often argued that temporary trade barriers are justified until infant industries mature. I believe the "infant industry" argument is valid, but in practice it has often been abused. Temporary trade barriers usually have eternal life, and the result is protection of inefficiently managed domestic industries.

As stated in Chapter 1, my program is committed to the principle of free trade and free international flow of capital. This is, as everyone understands, a very difficult principle to put into practice. The economic case for free trade is often overwhelmed by the interests of trade unions, short-sighted nationalism, or short-run political advantages. Unless politicians are prepared to accept personal sacrifices, if necessary, they will not be able to resist public demands for protectionist policies.

The traditional argument in favor of free trade has been the benefits of international specialization according to comparative advantages. The case for free trade has recently been augmented by Mancur Olson, who argued persuasively that free trade can prevent distributional coalitions (special-interest groups) from inefficiently distorting resource allocations. This theory has substantially enhanced the economic case for free trade, but it is not yet widely accepted. I believe, however, that free trade and free international flows of capital can benefit the human race in a more fundamental way: they can open a path leading to world survival. It is hoped that the political case for free trade presented below will help to soften the public resistance to it.

History teaches us that the commercial revolution in Western Europe necessitated and made possible jurisdictional integration of feudal fiefdoms into new nation states. The emergence of these nation states expedited the removal of local tariffs and other impediments to trade and the expansion of the market. Free flow of goods and services over a wider market area meant increased interaction among people from different localities and thus made jurisdictional integration durable. In other words, integration and free trade mutually reinforced each other and paved the way for the Industrial Revolution.

In the twentieth century, despite the restraints occasionally imposed by recurring protectionist sentiment, advances in communication and transportation technology facilitated a fairly rapid growth of international trade. There is no doubt that industrialized countries benefited from the growth of international trade. In addition, Japan rode the trade vehicle to catch up with Western Europe, and some of the developing countries, with the help of growing world trade, have emerged during the past two decades as newly industrializing countries (NICS). However, not everyone believes that free trade and free international flow of capital, particularly foreign direct investment by multinational corporations, will be beneficial to developing countries. As discussed earlier, some even view free trade and foreign direct investment of multinational corporations as vehicles of neocolonialism.

The Third World's hostility toward multinational corporations has some justification. Too often multinational corporations have ignored the values and aspirations of the local population either because of a mistaken belief that what was good for their companies was also good for the people of the host countries, or because of callousness. Multinationals' desire to maintain political stability in their host countries and their use of influence for that purpose often assisted political oppression that proved, in the end, to be counterproductive to their own interests. It is hoped that multinational corporations will learn from their past mistakes. Making friends with people of host countries is far superior to inviting hostilities. It must also be conceded that the abuses by multinational corporations were possible largely because corrupt governments of host countries allowed them in exchange for bribes.

Recognizing the transgressions of multinational corporations, however, should not inevitably lead to the conclusion that they are the agents of neocolonialism. No serious thinker can maintain that the Korean-owned plants in America are the agents of Korean imperialism preying on the helpless Americans. Despite the iniquities that could have and should have been avoided, multinational corporations do contribute significantly to the economic development process.

In my estimation, however, free trade and the spread of foreign direct investment, if accompanied by the investors' understanding of, and concurrence with, the aspirations of the people of the host countries, will benefit the world in a more fundamental way than just raising the standard of living. I believe these activities will facilitate the economic and, ultimately, political integration of the world and thus are essential to the survival of the human race. The European Common Market has contributed not only to the economic growth of the member nations but also to their security. With the present stockpile of nuclear weapons capable of annihilating the entire world many times over, we cannot afford to maintain our current international relations, which are characterized by contentious division. World integration is our historic mission, and we cannot afford to fail; the survival of the human race depends on it.

It will not be easy to take advantage of the opportunities provided by growing world trade and the spread of foreign direct investment. Governments will be tempted to erect trade barriers; the First World and its multinational corporations will be tempted to ignore the aspirations of the Third World; and the Third World will be tempted to blame others for its own mismanagement. Nor is overcoming these temptations enough to bring about world integration. The United States and its allies must provide leadership by bringing together countries with differing interests. It must be recognized that the Third World is not destined to serve the interest of the First World, which thus must strive to find ways to serve mutual interests while moving the world toward integration.

NOTES

1. One example has been to inflate the cost of plant construction so that government officials, business executives, and foreign suppliers can share the excess payment.
2. World Bank, *World Development Report 1981* (New York: Oxford University Press, 1981), 148–49.
3. Bank of Korea, *Economic Statistics Yearbook*, 1983, 7; and u.s. Government Printing Office, *Economic Report of the President*, 1982, 291.
4. The three most indebted nations were Brazil ($97 billion), Mexico ($83 billion), and Argentina ($42 billion). See *Wall Street Journal*, 11 April 1984.
5. *Dae Han Daily News*, 24 January 1984.
6. President Park was once so convincing that many people panicked and went on spending sprees. Among the less sophisticated people, the prevailing mood was to enjoy before North Korea attacked!
7. World Bank, *World Tables*, 3d ed., vol. 1, 1983.
8. See Charles R. Frank, Kwang Suk Kim, and Larry Westphal, *Foreign Trade Regimes and Economic Development: South Korea* (New York: National Bureau of Economic Research, 1975), 106–7.
9. It is doubtful that Korea's latest attempt to raise foreign capital through the New York Stock Exchange where the Korea Fund was introduced on 22 August 1984 will be successful. As long as Korea's political situation remains unchanged, American investors will shy away from the Korea Fund.
10. The Korean government and many Western observers maintain that Korea's foreign debt is manageable, because of her rapidly growing exports. However, Korea's export growth has so far been unable to erase the trade deficit and it is unlikely that Korea will enjoy a sizable trade surplus in the near future. Therefore, Korea's rising debt-service requirements will necessitate a painful choice between more borrowing (i.e., snowballing of the debt total) and draconian import restrictions (i.e., lowering the standard of living).

5

The problem of concentration

Concentration of income and wealth

To many Western observers, Korea's rapid economic growth since the early 1960s seems to have been achieved with a fairly equitable distribution of income. /Nevertheless, most Koreans complain about the growing gap between the rich and the poor./ Of course, such complaints are also heard in most other societies. However, the ordinary Koreans' resentment is far more intense than, say, that of the Americans. Have the Koreans been spoiled by rapid growth, so that they expect too much too soon, or are Korea's income distribution data misleading?

Table 5-1 compares household income distribution in Korea and selected other countries. It suggests that Korea's income distribution is indeed more equitable than that of other developing countries. The income share of the bottom 40 percent of Korean households (16.9 percent) is significantly higher than the corresponding figures for other developing nations and slightly better than that of the United States. The share of the top 20 percent in Korea is significantly lower than that in other developing countries, but higher than that in the developed countries. Even more remarkable is that the share of the top 10 percent in Korea, 27.5 percent, is not much higher than that in Japan and the United States, while in some other developing countries, the top 10 percent has as much as 40 to 50 percent of national income.

What do we make of these statistics? It is quite likely that income distribution is relatively more equitable in Korea than in many developing nations largely because Korea has a homogenous racial composition and a more equitable distribution of human capital.[1] It does not seem plausible, however, that Korea's income distribution is similar to that in the United States or Japan, as indicated by the official statistics. Those who have lived in either of those countries and in Korea can feel the difference in the relative income gaps. In fact, the Korea Development Institute (a government agency) has recently conceded that wage disparities among Korean workers are significantly wider than those found in other countries.[2]

The reliability of the data must be questioned. All income distribution data are subject to measurement errors. However, in the case of Korea, the income distribution data are systematically biased so that the measured distribution will appear to be more equal than in reality. Specifically, these

Table 5-1. National household income distribution (percent of total)

Country	Year	Bottom 20%	Next 20%	Next 40%	Top 20%	(Top 10%)
Korea	1976	5.7%	11.2%	37.8%	45.3%	(27.5%)
Indonesia	1976	6.6	7.8	36.2	49.4	(34.0)
Philippines	1970–71	5.2	9.0	31.8	54.0	(38.5)
Turkey	1973	3.4	8.0	32.0	56.5	(40.7)
Malaysia	1970	3.3	7.3	32.9	56.6	(39.6)
Mexico	1977	2.9	7.0	32.4	57.7	(40.6)
Brazil	1972	2.0	5.0	26.4	66.6	(50.6)
Argentina	1970	4.4	9.7	35.6	50.3	(35.2)
Venezuela	1970	3.0	7.3	35.7	54.0	(35.7)
United Kingdom	1977–78	7.4	11.7	41.7	39.5	(23.3)
Japan	1969	7.9	13.1	38.0	41.0	(27.2)
Sweden	1972	6.6	13.1	43.3	37.0	(21.3)
United States	1972	4.5	10.7	42.0	42.8	(26.6)

Source: World Bank, *World Development Report 1981*, 182–83.

data are derived from surveys that exclude wealthy households, single-person households, nonfarm households in rural areas, and small farmers.[3] Such exclusions of the households at both ends of the distribution would obviously result in a measured distribution with relatively smaller dispersion. If the bias is small, the data may still be useful so long as the direction and the likely magnitude of the bias are recognized. However, the survey results that show the average rural income in Korea to be higher than the average urban income are inconsistent with the massive flight of farmers from rural to urban areas (see Chapter 7) and with other indicators of Korea's rural economy and thus are not very useful for international comparison.

Nevertheless, the same survey results can be useful for determining *changes over time*. And in this regard, the evidence is discouraging. According to the official income-distribution data, the income share of Korea's bottom 40 percent *dropped* from 19.3 percent in 1965 to 16.1 percent in 1980, while the share of top 20 percent *rose* from 41.8 percent to 45.4 percent during the same period.[4] These are sizable changes for income-distribution data. Since it is unlikely that the bias in the data has been reduced over time, deterioration of income distribution in Korea appears to have been quite serious.[5]

There are no reliable data for the distribution of wealth in Korea. However, one recent survey of housing values suggests a polarization (see Table 5-2). Instead of the typical bell-shaped distribution, Korea's housing-value distribution is characterized by a heavy concentration at the lower

Table 5-2. U.S. and Korean distributions of owner-occupied housing values

Korea[a] (1983)		United States[b] (1980)	
Property value	Percent	Property value	Percent
Less than $12,500	68	Less than $20,000	8.1
$12,500 – $25,000	21	$20,000 – $25,000	4.5
$25,000 – $37,500	5	$25,000 – $35,000	12.7
$37,500 – $62,500	1	$35,000 – $50,000	23.2
$62,500–$112,500	0	Over $50,000	51.5
Over $112,500	5		

Source: National Land Development Research Institute, Seoul (as reported in *The Minjoong Shinmoon*, 16 December 1983); U.S. Department of Commerce, *Statistical Abstract of the United States*, 1982–1983, 753.
a. For the eleven largest cities only.
b. For the entire United States.

end. In contrast with the United States, where housing values exhibit a more normal distribution, Korea's housing values show that the middle class is virtually nonexistent.

Concentration of market power

The economic policies of the Park and Chun regimes, which widened the gap between the rich and the poor, have also widened the gap between large conglomerates and smaller corporations. Despite the (misleading) assertion that dictatorship provides a strong government, a crucial weakness of the Park–Chun dictatorship has been its inability to reverse the trend toward ever-increasing market power of giant conglomerates and ever-worsening distribution of income and wealth.

As Table 5-3 demonstrates, a handful of giant conglomerates came to account for an increasingly large portion of Korea's GDP in the late 1970s. The same trend has accelerated since President Chun Doo Hwan took over the government with a vow to continue his predecessor's economic policy zealously. For example, sales of the ten largest conglomerates, which in 1981 amounted to 42.8 percent of that year's GNP, rose to 57.1 percent of GNP in 1982 and to 65.2 percent in 1983.[6] The magnitude of change in the last two years is, to say the least, extraordinary.[7] In the United States, by contrast, the sales of the ten largest corporations amounted to only 15.8 percent of GNP in 1983.[8] Further evidence of the concentration trend in Korea is that the share of total exports attributed to the ten largest exporters rose from 12.4 percent in 1975 to 48.7 percent in 1982[9] and it further increased to 70 percent in 1984.[10]

Table 5-3. Value-added by large corporations
(percent of GDP)

Number of Corporations	1975	1976	1977	1978
5 Largest corporations	4.7	5.1	8.2	8.1
10 Largest corporations	7.1	7.2	10.6	10.9
20 Largest corporations	9.8	9.4	13.3	14.0
46 Largest corporations	12.3	12.3	16.3	17.1

Source: Il Sakong, *Economic Growth and Concentration of Economic Power* (Seoul: Korea Development Institute, 1980), 5.

The main reason for the rapid concentration of economic power in Korea is the collaboration of the political and economic powers. In Korea, the government can decide the fate of any business firm, and the economy is centrally planned. Planning in Korea, of course, is not the type used in a command economy. However, the enormous power of the government is simply too strong for any private business firm to resist. For example, in 1982, when the government decided to sell off the commercial banks it owned, it had selected buyers in advance and prearranged bid prices by all potential buyers. No one was allowed to foil the government plan, and as a result commercial banks are now owned by a handful of giant conglomerates that already controlled a vast network of manufacturing, distribution, exports, and services. Korea's banks under President Park used to be subservient to the needs of large corporations. Under President Chun, banks have become members of giant conglomerates! As a result, 20.8 percent of total outstanding bank loans went to the ten largest conglomerates by the first half of 1983.[11] The situation has worsened considerably since then; by March 1984 nearly one-quarter (24.2 percent) of total outstanding bank credits had gone to the five largest conglomerates.[12]

The pace of concentration has so accelerated in recent years that the giant conglomerates are now vertically integrated in the production and distribution of a vast array of goods and services; thus, they have greatly reduced their functional interdependency with smaller firms. As a result, only 18 percent of Korea's small or medium-sized firms received contracts from large corporations; the corresponding figure in Japan is 60.7 percent. Only 24 percent of Korea's 3,800 export firms were small businesses (defined as those with less than $1 million of annual exports) in 1982, while 96 percent of Taiwan's 70,000 export firms were small businesses.[13] Small and medium-sized manufacturing firms in Korea accounted for only 32 percent of the total national value of shipments, compared with 52 percent in Japan and 65 percent in Taiwan.[14] These statistics imply that Korea's small or medium-sized firms are not complementary to large corporations but in competition with them.

The extent of concentration is especially serious in manufacturing and mining. According to recently released official data, the five largest conglomerates in 1981 accounted for 21.5 percent of the total value of shipments in mining and manufacturing, up from 15.9 percent in 1978, while the corresponding figure for the sixteenth to thirtieth largest conglomerates *declined* from 7.6 percent to 7.1 percent over the same period. In addition, of the 2,257 major manufactured goods studied, 87.8 percent were found to be supplied by monopolistic or oligopolistic firms.[15] Since all available indicators indicate acceleration of the concentration trend during the past three years, the extent of concentration of market power at present must be much more serious than it was in 1981.

Causes of concentration

What are the main causes of the concentration of income and market power in Korea? Is it an inevitable result of economic development that will reverse itself as the Korean economy continues its progress? That is the implication of the so-called "inverted-U" model, according to which the degree of inequality in income distribution increases initially as the economy grows and later decreases as the economy passes a certain stage of development. This may indeed have been the typical pattern observed in the past, but I do not believe it is in any sense a natural or inevitable course of economic development. There is no theoretical reason for accepting a serious deterioration of the income distribution and concentration of market power as an unavoidable outcome of developmental process.

One important reason for the deterioration of income distribution in Korea has been the government's low-wage and anti-labor policies. Ostensibly for the purpose of preserving international competitiveness, the Korean government has consciously attempted to hold wages down.[16] For the low-wage policy to be successful, however, market forces must be interfered with; otherwise wages will increase commensurately with the rise in labor productivity. The government's interference with market forces for the purpose of holding wages down is what I refer to as anti-labor policy. The tools of anti-labor policy range from bureaucratic harassment and intimidation to the use of terror and imprisonment in order to discourage job actions and labor movements.[17]

As a result of the low-wage policy, the average real wage rose by only 3.07 percent per year from 1970 to 1981, compared with a growth in labor productivity of 11.5 percent per year (see Table 5-4). The low-wage policy is still alive; in 1983, the third year of economic expansion, when labor productivity rose 12.5 percent, real wages increased by only 8.3 percent, and for 1984, when real GNP is supposed to grow by 7.5 percent according to the government plan, the government recommended a wage freeze to private industries. Since the government carries a big stick, this recommendation cannot easily be ignored.

Table 5-4. Average annual growth rates of real wages and productivity (percent)

Period	Labor productivity[a]	Real wages[b]
1970–81	11.50	3.07
1975–81	8.62	2.11

Source: Calculated from the data given by the Ministry of Labor, as cited in *Korea in 1982* (New York: Galilee Moongo, 1983), 67, and the Bank of Korea, *Economic Statistics Yearbook*, 1983.
a. Defined as nonagricultural output per employee in real terms.
b. Defined as monthly earnings of regular employees (including management-level employees) divided by the minimum cost of living for a four-person urban household.

The most important reason for the concentration of market power is the inevitable corruption of a dictatorial government due to the lack of institutional checks and balances. In addition, in a modern noncommunist state that needs to maintain some semblance of democracy by holding elections (however manipulated they are), a dictatorial government needs to cultivate big businesses as its main sources of political funds. One piece of evidence that the giant conglomerates benefit from the symbiotic relationship with the government is that, as of December 1983, 62.5 percent of the monopolistic or oligopolistic markets were protected by import restrictions, as opposed to only 19.6 percent for the Korean market as a whole. In addition, for those commodities without import restrictions, the average tariff rate for the monopolistic or oligopolistic markets was 41.5 percent— 17.8 percentage points higher than the overall average of 23.7 percent.[18]

The concentration of market power into a handful of giant conglomerates has reached such an extreme that a recent article in the *Wall Street Journal* (13 April 1983) described Korea's five-year economic development plan as a government-drafted plan that charts the way for the country's *nine huge industrial conglomerates*. Such concentration of market power has caused many serious socioeconomic problems. For example, if a smaller firm is fortunate enough to obtain a contract from a large conglomerate, it must pay cash for its raw material, but is invariably paid in return by three-to-six-month promissory notes. This is a very difficult burden for smaller firms with constant cash-flow problems, but they have no alternative. Moreover, they are fortunate if contract prices are not slashed before payment.

Recently it was reported that eighteen of the twenty construction companies examined by the Fair Trade Commission (including the ten largest) had been found guilty of unfair trade practices, including delay of payment to the subcontractors and unfairly slashing the subcontracting prices.[19] These violators include concerns belonging to the ten largest conglomerates, such as Hyundai, Samsung, Daewoo, Lotte, and Daelim. Among these, the country's biggest construction company, belonging to the number one conglomerate, was found to have most frequently abused market power by unfairly cutting subcontractor prices, although it had been warned by the Commission a year before. Such unfair practices will no doubt continue so long as the government cannot be voted out, since it has been the standard practice of the government to publicize its "warnings" for propaganda purposes and do nothing about them afterward.

Thus, small or medium-sized firms have to contend not only with discriminatory credit rationing but also with financial abuses by the bigger corporations. Such double jeopardy is in itself unfortunate, but its economic consequences are even worse. The first and most obvious undesirable economic consequence of the concentration is that the consumers must pay higher prices for poorer-quality commodities than they would in a competitive market. For example, a recent Economic Planning Board study of twenty monopolistic or oligopolistic markets found that the domestic prices in these markets were over 50 percent higher than the world market prices.[20]

Another important economic consequence of the concentration of market power is the worsening income distribution. As shown in Table 5-5, small or medium-sized firms in 1982 had higher value-added/sales ratios than large firms. In addition, small or medium-sized firms devoted a smaller portion of their value-added to depreciation allowances than did large firms, enjoyed higher profit margins, and at the same time paid out a larger portion of value-added for wages and salaries. Since Korea's small or medium-sized firms are not complementary to large conglomerates but in competition with them, promoting the growth of small or medium-sized firms would increase the share of wages and salaries in total value-added and thus improve income distribution.

An interesting consequence of Korea's concentration trend can be found in the fact that Taiwan, which has much less economic concentration, is

Table 5-5. Value-added/sales ratios and compositions of value-added, by firm size, 1982

	Large firms	Small or medium-sized firms
Value-added/sales	18.2%	23.4%
Composition of value-added		
Profits	4.6%	12.7%
Wages and salaries	46.6	61.2
Financing costs	26.2	12.5
Depreciation, etc.	22.6	13.6

Source: Association of Small or Medium-Sized Firms, as cited in Dong-
    A Ilbo, 3 February 1984.

rapidly moving ahead in its competition against Korea. For example, in the latest listing of the 500 largest non-American corporations, five Korean conglomerates (ranked 37 to 64) made the top 100 list in contrast to only one (ranked 81) for Taiwan.[21] In addition, Korea had ten conglomerates among the top 250, while Taiwan had only three (ranked 81, 202, and 472) in the entire International 500 list. Despite such size differences between the conglomerates of the two economies, Taiwan's total exports from January to July 1984 ($19.1 billion) exceeded that of Korea by $2.7 billion.[22] Furthermore, Taiwan's per capita GNP in 1983 ($2,673) exceeded that of Korea ($1,884) by 41.9 percent, significantly up from a 9.4 percent difference in 1978.

Why is Korea falling so fast behind Taiwan? One important reason is the inefficiency of Korea's conglomerates. Korea's large conglomerates rely on various incentives and protection to stay in business. They are not as efficient as their smaller competitors that survive despite numerous obstacles. The main reason for the large conglomerates' relative inefficiency is that they are not specialized, whereas their smaller competitors are specialized in one line of business or a few related activities. Even the largest corporation in the world, Exxon, is specialized in energy (though it is also engaged in other *minor* activities), and most of the American giant corporations have specialized business activities. In contrast, Korea's conglomerates are involved in almost every field, ranging from heavy industry, chemicals, and light manufacturing to distribution, department stores, banking, securities, and insurance. Therefore, concentration of market power not only hinders efficient use of resources but also worsens income distribution, since large firms tend to use more capital-intensive methods of production because their financing costs are relatively low.

Measures for reducing the concentration of income and market power

As stated in Chapter 1, true economic development requires that all groups—workers, entrepreneurs, farmers, and consumers—be given equal opportunity to participate fully in production and sharing of goods and services. To ensure such development, the government must refrain from looking after the interests of the privileged groups. The Park and Chun governments' belief that rapid economic growth can be achieved by helping big businesses is misguided and immoral. More specific recommendations are discussed below.

First, to improve income distribution in Korea, the misguided low-wage, anti-labor policy must be abolished. Since unskilled low-wage workers are most frequently exploited by monopsonistic employers, protecting the rights of these workers will increase their welfare. Even if the abolition of the low-wage, anti-labor policy did not improve income distribution significantly, the low-income workers would not feel betrayed by their own government. Therefore, the government should act as an impartial arbitrator and must strive to promote harmonious labor–management relations.

Second, the economy of rural areas must be improved. The great disparity between the living standards of urban and rural areas not only contributes to income inequality but also creates other social problems. Policy measures to improve rural economies will be discussed in Chapter 7.

Third, all forms of discrimination should be removed, since it violates the principle of "equal opportunity for all groups." The education system that favors the schools in the wealthy urban neighborhoods will perpetuate inequality in income. Discrimination in the labor market based on a person's sex or regional origin not only promotes income inequality but also results in a waste of human resources. While some redistributive measures may tend to hinder efficient allocation of resources, removal of discrimination improves both efficiency and equality at the same time.

Discrimination against women in the labor market is a particularly wasteful element in Korea's manpower use. Each year, a large number of women graduate from high schools and colleges but their career opportunities are extremely limited. As a result, only a small number of women, mostly young and unmarried, participate in the labor force. Furthermore, most women in the labor force are working or looking for jobs out of desperation. While 44 percent of the married women with no more than six years of education participated in the labor force in 1980, the labor-force-participation rates were only 22.4 percent, 16.6 percent, and 28 percent, respectively, for those with nine years and twelve years of education, and for college graduates.[23]

Women who do find work face further discrimination in the workplace. Their average monthly pay in 1982 was only 44 percent of the average monthly pay for male workers, despite the fact that women worked longer (237.8 hours per month) than men (228.9 hours per month).[24] Women's role in the workplace is also restricted. A recent survey by the Ministry of Labor showed that 73.3 percent of working women were employed in manufacturing industries, in contrast to 21.1 percent for all men and women, and 70.2 percent of the employed women were production workers (almost all of them young girls).[25] According to a recent study by the Korean Institute for Women, one-third of the ninety-two corporations it surveyed had internal rules with discriminatory hiring, promotion, and remuneration standards, and most others with no such written regulations also practiced sex discrimination.[26] Such sex discrimination results in a waste of educational expenditures, even after allowing for the social value of educated homemakers and mothers.

Fourth, large conglomerates should not be given preferential consideration in credit allocation. Instead, financial markets must be allowed to operate completely free of government interference in credit allocation and interest-rate determination, and the Antitrust Division of the Ministry of Justice ought to scrutinize business takeovers and prevent the Pac-Man-like gobbling-up of small businesses by larger corporations if those takeovers will reduce efficiency. In addition, the government ought to provide a fair business climate to small or medium-sized firms so that they can overcome the disadvantages in financing. As shown in Table 5-5, small or medium-sized firms tend to use relatively more labor-intensive techniques than large corporations, thus, the growth of small or medium-sized firms will create more employment opportunities than the growth of large corporations, thereby improving income distribution. Moreover, small or medium-sized firms tend to be more dynamic and creative, whereas large corporations suffer from bureaucratic inertia. Therefore, government policy favoring large corporations is counterproductive, and assisting small or medium-sized businesses is justified in economic terms, and not simply because it is morally satisfying to help underdogs.

Fifth, the government ought to use tax incentives to make the ownership of conglomerates open to the public and to encourage ordinary citizens to invest in these corporations. Whereas the large corporations of the United States, Japan, and other developed countries are owned by hundreds of thousands of shareholders, each of Korea's conglomerates is owned almost exclusively by one family. This is one important reason why the conglomerates are so hated by the Korean people. If the ordinary people were allowed to own pieces of these corporations, the business community and the citizenry as a whole would cultivate more harmonious relations and thus increase social stability.

Sixth, for those conglomerates that have already gained effective control over the markets, free trade will provide them with tough foreign competition. This will not only be beneficial to consumers but also improve economic efficiency in the long run.

Finally, to lighten the tax burden of low-income households, a major overhaul of the tax system must be implemented. The current tax system, which relies on regressive indirect taxes for over 70 percent of government revenues, is grossly unfair. To promote a more equitable tax burden, most of the indirect taxes should be replaced by direct taxes, including a progressive consumption tax (see Chapter 8).

All of the above measures will help improve the distribution of income in Korea. However, the ultimate solution lies in institutionalizing democratic political processes that, through the mechanism of checks and balances, will prevent large-scale corruption and collaboration between economic and political powers, and provide equal opportunity for full participation of all groups in the sharing of the benefits of economic growth. Under a succession of dictators, it has been difficult for the Korean public to learn about the economic abuses of government and unscrupulous businessmen. Even when some problems were exposed, little could be done because the executive branch had a monopoly of political power. If Korea had had a democratic government with separation of powers and freedom of press, its economic situation would be much better than it is now.

NOTES

1. See Chapter 9.
2. *Dong-A Ilbo*, 4 July 1984. The article was based on a recent KDI report, "Changes in Wage Distribution in Korea during the 1970s" (Seoul, 1984).
3. See Paul W. Kuznets, *Economic Growth and Structure in the Republic of Korea* (New Haven: Yale University Press, 1977), 97.
4. *Dong-A Ilbo*, 28 April 1983.
5. Manipulation of data for political purposes has been standard practice in Korea. For example, in the mid-1970s the Economic Planning Board used, for its calculation of the CPI, the retail price of rice, which was lower than the wholesale price; when the price of Chinese cabbage skyrocketed in 1978, it was simply excluded from the market basket! Given this inclination of the Korean government, it is very likely that it had done its best to *improve* the income-distribution data. The published data nevertheless show deterioration of the distribution, and reality is likely to be worse.
6. *Dong-A Ilbo*, 31 December 1983 and 22 August 1984. Korea's data are strongly understated because the conglomerates' control over many companies is disguised. A recent government report showed that the number of companies under the disguised control of the conglomerates was at least 25 percent of the number that had been known previously, and there might be many more that could not be identified. See *Dong-A Ilbo*, 14 April 1984.
7. Gross sales value cannot be directly compared to GNP, which is total value-added, but their growth rates may be compared. The rise in the ratio of sales to GNP, therefore, indicates that the ten largest conglomerates accounted for a growing portion of the GNP.
8. *New York Times*, 12 March 1984.
9. *Dong-A Ilbo*, 31 July 1983.
10. *New York Times*, 4 January 1985.
11. Ministry of Finance's Report to the National Assembly (11 November 1983), as reported in *Dong-A Ilbo*, 11 November 1983.
12. *Dong-A Ilbo*, 22 August 1984.
13. *Dong-A Ilbo*, 15 June 1983.
14. *Dong-A Ilbo*, 28 January 1984.
15. *Dong-A Ilbo*, 27 April 1984. The Economic Planning Board released these statistics. For statistical purposes, oligopoly is defined as the market situation in which over 50 percent of an industry's total supply is attributable to three or fewer firms.
16. According to a recent article in the *Wall Street Journal* (13 April 1984), "There is a conscious government policy to hold wages down to help make [Korean] exports competitive."
17. In a letter of protest sent to the prime minister, the Church and Society Committee of the Korean National Council of Churches demanded, among other things, that the government refrain from black-listing union activists and modify its generally hostile approach to labor. See *Sae Gae Times*, 28 January 1984.
18. *Dong-A Ilbo*, 29 December 1983.
19. *Dong-A Ilbo*, 13 January 1984.
20. *Dae-Han Daily News*, 31 January 1984.
21. *Fortune*, 20 August 1984, 202–13.
22. *Dong-A Ilbo*, 10 September 1984.
23. These census data are cited from S. K. Kim and K. O. Shim, "An Analysis of the Determinants of the Korean Women's Labor Force Participation" (Seoul: Korea Development Institute, 1984).
24. *Dae-Han Daily News*, 31 July 1984.
25. *The Minjoong Shinmoon*, 13 April 1984.
26. *Dong-A Ilbo*, 22 February 1984.

6

Labor relations policy

The cross of a low-wage policy

The Park and Chun administrations have brutally suppressed any labor activity not authorized by the government. The stated purpose of this anti-labor policy is to hold wages down in order to keep Korean exports competitive. Whether government intervention in market functions can actually succeed in holding wages down is not self-evident (to be discussed later). The Korean government has acted in the misguided belief that its anti-labor policy would be successful in keeping Korean products *competitive* in the international market. Thus, Korea's labor, which has had no reputation for militancy, has been unfairly forced to carry the cross of a low-wage policy.

A dictatorial government cannot tolerate independent labor unions because they might become powerful opposition forces. Apart from the political reasons for the anti-labor policy, the government's allegation of a need to keep wages low may appear plausible at first glance, but it will be found seriously flawed upon closer examination. During the early stage of industrialization of Korea, surplus labor that was relatively well-educated but unskilled because of a lack of experience was abundantly available. Korea was able to tap this resource at low cost. However, as continued industrialization fully absorbed unskilled cheap labor by the early 1970s, wages began to rise. In other words, the Korean economy, which had been expanding by increasing the *quantity* of input, passed into a new phase in which availability of cheap labor can no longer be counted on.

A natural response to the market signal of rising wages would be to improve the *quality* of input and thus compete on the basis of high productivity instead of cheap labor. Unfortunately, President Park chose to use physical force to keep wages low rather than to offset wage increases by productivity increases, and President Chun has adopted an even tougher anti-labor policy than his predecessor.

Can the government hold wages down despite upward market pressure on wages? Through wage and price controls, it may be able to keep nominal and real wages low in the short run. However, in a *competitive* labor market, real wage growth cannot be held below productivity growth in the long run. Nevertheless, real wage growth may be held below productivity growth if the labor market becomes *less competitive* over time because the market power of the employers increases. The increase in market power of the

47

Table 6-1. Firm size and wage increase, 1984[a]

Size	100–299	300–499	500–999	Over 1,000
Wage increase	6.36%	5.47%	4.90%	4.54%

Source: Ministry of Labor (as reported in the Dong-A Ilbo, 17 May 1984).
a. Firm size is measured by the number of employees.

Korean employers has been facilitated by business takeovers and the government's low-wage, anti-labor policy. The result has been, as shown in Table 5-4, a slower growth in real wages than in labor productivity. Table 6-1 shows the wage increase data for 1984, a year when a continuation of normal economic growth was expected. The larger the company, the smaller the wage increases, contrary to the pattern observed in the developed countries. This perverse phenomenon implies that as the firm gets bigger, the bargaining power of management increases because of increased suppression of labor by the government.

The increase in the Korean employers' market power has also been facilitated by the government policy of consciously favoring large conglomerates. The evidence presented in the preceding chapter indicates that the share of GNP accruing to the ten largest conglomerates has increased by more than 50 percent during the last three years. Thus, anti-labor policy and the increasing concentration of the market power into fewer and larger corporations have together resulted in wage increases that lagged behind the productivity increases, as shown in Table 5-4.

Another way in which the government can influence real wages in the long run is to influence labor productivity. If the low-wage policy results in a slowdown of productivity growth, its long-run consequence will be a slowdown of real wage growth. This cannot be the intended result of the low-wage policy, but, as I will demonstrate below, it is the inevitable consequence.

Slower productivity growth

The adverse effects of wage increases can be offset by productivity increases. Therefore, if excess demand for labor results in an increase in wages, which in turn makes Korean exports less competitive, Korea's employers will be forced to seek measures to increase the productivity of their workers. However, employers will have weaker incentive to improve labor productivity if they believe they can count on the government in their attempt to keep labor costs down. In the American steel industry, for example, steel makers have long neglected labor productivity because they knew that import restrictions would enable them to pass on cost increases to the buyers.

Because of the limited size of the domestic market, Korean firms survive mainly by selling their products abroad. Thus, they cannot rely on import

Table 6-2. Unemployment rate by education level, 1982

Education level	Less than 6 years	6 to 8 years	9 to 11 years	12 to 15 years	16 years or more
Unemployment rate	0.5%	2.3%	4.8%	8.0%	6.0%

Source: Economic Planning Board (as reported in *Dong-A Ilbo*, 19 January 1984).

restrictions when their products become less competitive. They must stay competitive. Without the low-wage policy, Korean firms will have no choice but to seek productivity growth. But if there is a reasonable assurance that the government will use whatever means necessary to keep wages low, employers are likely to become complacent. Ironically, the low-wage policy will succeed in holding wages down by keeping productivity growth down. Of course, such a result defeats the purpose of the low-wage policy, since the benefit of low wages will be offset by poor productivity growth.

Table 6-2 statistically demonstrates the long-run consequence of the low-wage policy. In 1982 uneducated low-wage workers had the lowest unemployment rate, and the unemployment rate of high-school graduates (the pool of skilled blue-collar workers) was the highest. Since the Korean economy in 1982 was still operating below full capacity, one would expect a higher unemployment rate for the unskilled than the skilled labor force. Contrary to this expectation, the higher the education level, the higher was the unemployment rate, except for the college graduates, who are mostly employed at the management level or by the government.

Further evidence of the productivity consequences of the low-wage policy has been recently documented by Kim, Ryu, and Hwang.[1] Their study finds that productivity growth in Korea accounts for only 23.6 percent of the manufacturing output growth from 1967 to 1979, while the remainder of output growth is attributable to increases in the quantities of labor and capital inputs. This figure compares quite unfavorably to 32.4 percent for Taiwan and 49.4 percent for Japan. Despite two decades of rapid economic growth, therefore, the Korean economy is still relying on the low-skill, low-technology industries. This is a reflection of the low-wage, low-technology bias in the government's industrial policy.

Hostile labor–management relations

The productivity short-fall resulting from the low-wage policy may be recovered, given time and proper policy changes.[2] However, hostile labor–management relations fostered by the anti-labor policy will have a lasting and negative effect on the country's economic efficiency, and thus are potentially more damaging than the productivity loss. As discussed in Chapter 1, there is a good reason to expect Korea's labor–management relations to be as cooperative as those of Japan. Unfortunately, the government's short-sighted actions have repeatedly angered the workers, who are likely to become militant if the government continues its attempt to subjugate them.

An example will show how the workers are treated in Korea. When young female workers of Dong-Il Textile Company waged a sit-in in 1976 demanding an improvement of working conditions, policemen broke in and beat them up with clubs without making any attempt to conduct an investigation. These girls were then summarily fired without due process and blacklisted. They have not been able to find jobs to this day. Incidents like this have been too numerous to list here. One labor leader, Chun Tae-Il, even burned himself to death in protest against the callousness of the government in handling his repeated efforts to improve the working conditions of the Peace Market garment district. The use of violence by the government, which has a moral and legal obligation to uphold law and order, can never be justified.

Developing nations can benefit from the experiences of the developed countries; those that proved to be helpful to economic development may be emulated and mistakes can be avoided. Korea should not be emulating the adversary labor–management relationship found in the United Kingdom and the United States. It is now well recognized in the West that Japan's cooperative labor–management relationship is responsible for superior productivity growth of the Japanese economy. Since Korea's cultural heritage is similar to that of Japan, Korea would have no difficulty in adopting the Japanese-style cooperative labor–management relationship. However, the government and management should not use cooperation as an excuse for subjugating labor. Regrettably, such has been the case under the Park and Chun regimes, and the situation will not change until a democratic government is firmly instituted.

Chun's labor-law amendment: from bad to worse

Korea's labor laws were revised several times by President Park so as to make unionization more difficult than before. As a result, workers have had no freedom to organize independent unions. All unions must be approved by the government and are subject to frequent interventions on behalf of management. The procedures for collective bargaining involve so many obstacles that it is virtually impossible. Furthermore, all elections of union officers have been manipulated by the Korean CIA (now the Security Planning Agency), which has never been hesitant to use terror, violence, and imprisonment.

Not satisfied with existing legislation, President Chun recently made further changes. One amendment was to disallow national or industrywide unions. Only those organized at the company level may be approved. This change is, of course, aimed at preventing the emergence of powerful labor unions that might become strong political forces. However, the unfortunate consequence of this amendment is that Korea's labor unions will be fragmented. If they eventually regain freedom under a democratic government, these fragmented unions will contribute to economic inefficiency.

While labor unions are needed to prevent exploitation of the workers, it must also be recognized that, if they put their self-interest above the interest of the entire nation, powerful and militant unions will hinder efficient operation of an economy. As Mancur Olson demonstrates, fragmented unions tend to put their self-interest above the interest of the entire nation. For them to sacrifice self-interest is to lose too much for too little gain. On the other hand, for an encompassing union composed of a significantly large group of workers, national interest and self-interest may coincide, and it is less likely that the greed of union members will hurt the economy. For this reason, Korea's labor laws ought to be revised; encompassing unions must not only be allowed but also encouraged.

Trade dependency: revisited

Chapter 4 argued that the Korean economy is excessively dependent on international trade and that trade dependency must be reduced, not by reducing the volume of trade but by expanding the domestic market. To do that, the linkage between the export sector and the domestic sector must be enhanced (to be discussed in Chapter 7) and the purchasing power of the working class and the rural households must be increased.

As shown in the preceding chapter, there is a wide gap between the rich and the poor, and the middle class is almost nonexistent in Korea. Since the rich tend to satisfy their consumption needs by purchasing imported goods and the poor by purchasing domestic products, increasing the purchasing power of the working class and rural households will increase the demand for domestic products. This is a better policy than protecting domestic industries by import restriction. To improve the purchasing power of the working class, the misguided low-wage policy must be abolished.

Unsafe workplaces

The practice of awarding contracts and licenses in exchange for bribes and kickbacks, and the low-technology, low-wage bias in industrial policy have created an environment in which profits are made by cutting corners. The most dramatic example of such practices was the infamous collapse of the Wawoo Apartments in 1970. The apartments, financed by the city of Seoul, collapsed within a few months of completion, and hundreds of people were injured or killed. Only recently, Seoul's subway construction sites collapsed twice within two months. One serious economic consequence of cutting corners has been a steady rise in workplace accidents and work-related injuries, deaths, and diseases.

As shown in Table 6-3, the number of work-related injuries and deaths has been steadily increasing, except in 1980 when the recession slowed down manufacturing, mining, and construction activities. Furthermore, the Min-

Table 6-3. Work-related injuries and deaths and economic losses[a]

Year	1979	1980	1981	1982	1983
Injuries and deaths (percent of employees)	3.61%	3.02%	3.41%	3.98%	3.98%
Economic losses (percent of GNP)	0.93%	0.91%	0.90%	1.01%	1.11%

Source: Ministry of Labor (as reported in *Dae-Han Daily News*, 19 April 1984).
a. The data cover establishments with ten or more employees.

istry of Labor admits that if establishments with fewer than ten employees were included, the total numbers of injuries and deaths would be significantly higher than those shown in Table 6-3; for 1983, the number was estimated to be 317,000 (4.5 percent of total workers), with a total economic loss of 1,263.9 billion won (2.4 percent of GNP).

The trend shown in Table 6-3 testifies to the worsening of occupational safety records. Even after allowing for the growing size of the workforce, the number of work-related injuries and deaths has been on the rise. This trend reflects the cavalier attitude of the government about environmental and occupational safety, which is well illustrated by the Korean CIA's interrogation in 1970 of a professor who found serious water pollution in the vicinity of an industrial city. His crime was making his finding public; his research paper was denied circulation.

Running out of excuses for tyrannical actions, the Korean government felt economic growth might somehow be used as an acceptable excuse. Economic growth could not be slowed down for long-run intangible benefits like a cleaner environment and safe workplaces. But the chickens are coming home to roost. An ever-increasing number of miners, textile workers, and chemical workers are suffering from occupation-related diseases.[3]

Toward a fair labor policy

I am an advocate of a free-market economic system in which both labor and management are free to organize to protect their interests. Under Park and Chun, however, only management has had freedom, and the rights of workers have been thoroughly abridged. Workers' participation has been limited to the production of goods and services, and they have been denied their fair share of the fruits of their hard work. The results of this anti-labor, low-wage policy have been, as argued above, a slowdown of productivity growth and a festering hostility of workers toward management. These results must be reversed by a fair and compassionate labor policy that guarantees the rights of labor as well as those of management. Specifically, current labor laws have to be revised so that basic rights of workers are guaranteed and protected by the government.

Recognizing and guaranteeing the rights of labor, however, does not mean that labor can do no wrong. Selfishness of labor is just as damaging to national well-being as the selfishness of short-sighted businessmen. To prevent excessive power of potentially divisive and selfish labor unions, an encompassing labor union should be encouraged and fostered by offering economic incentives.

The most important element determining the long-run economic success of the country is, in my view, a harmonious and cooperative labor–management relationship. Short-sighted neglect of the workers' needs by management and equally short-sighted hostility of workers are damaging to both sides. What is bad for the company is bad for the employees, *and vice versa*. Labor and management are in the same boat. Recognition of this fact is essential to realizing full participation of all groups. The government, therefore, has a moral obligation to promote harmonious and cooperative labor–management relations by playing a constructive role as an impartial but interested arbitrator. Any temptation to side with either management or labor must be resisted. In addition, permitting and encouraging national or industrywide unions would be conducive to responsible union actions.

Finally, the importance of safe workplaces cannot be exaggerated. The loss of human capital due to work-related injuries and deaths cannot be compensated by short-run increases in output, for the economic might of a country, as discussed earlier, depends ultimately on human resources. Moreover, the value of life and limb must be held above short-lived economic gains. Occupational safety should therefore be vigorously pursued to the extent that safety requirements do not impose excessive burdens on business firms.

NOTES

1. Y. K. Kim, J. S. Ryu, and K. H. Hwang, "An Analysis of Manufacturing Productivity in Korea, Taiwan and Japan," Han Yang University, Economic Research Center (Seoul, 1984).
2. Output foregone in the meantime will never be recouped.
3. The number of miners suffering from lung diseases rose from less than 1,000 in 1978 to 2,379 in 1981 and 2,724 in 1982. See *Dong-A Ilbo*, 6 February 1984.

7

Interregional and intersectoral imbalances: problems and solutions

Interregional imbalance

The problem

Perhaps the most dramatic aspect of the interregional imbalance of the Korean economy is the fact that the city of Seoul, which accounts for only 0.6 percent of total land area, has nearly a quarter of the total population, 64 percent of total bank deposits, 54 percent of all automobiles, 45 percent of the color television sets, and 43 percent of the nation's college students.[1] Every year, great numbers of people move into Seoul, and all major cultural, educational, commercial, industrial, and governmental bodies are located there. If one wants to succeed in business, art, or *any* career, Seoul is the place to do it. And to give a good education to his children, one must go to Seoul. In a country that is already heavily populated (over four hundred persons per square kilometer, or over one thousand persons per square mile), increasing concentration of population and related activities in Seoul has taxed the city's infrastructure and municipal services beyond their limits.

As shown in Table 7-1, the growth of Korea's urban population during the past two decades has been relatively fast, and the concentration of urban population in the largest city is excessively high by international standards. The fact that urbanization proceeds commensurately with economic development is not, of course, an unusual phenomenon. But Seoul is an extreme case which has evolved over three decades because of its special circumstance, i.e., authoritarian dictatorship with no allowance for local autonomy. Every major decision is made in Seoul, and heads of provincial and local governments who are appointed by the president merely execute directives received from above. Under such circumstances, it would be wise indeed for ambitious persons to be in Seoul.

Nevertheless, not everything can be done in Seoul. Of the manufacturing facilities and infrastructure not located in Seoul, the home region of Presidents Park and Chun, the Yungnam, has received much more than its share. The Korean people say that the Honam region gets bad deals, and the Choongchung region gets no deal at all from the government. Such regional discrimination is detrimental to national unity and thus threatens

Table 7-1. International comparison of urbanization

Country	Urban population as percent of total population 1960	1980	Percent of urban population in largest city 1960	1980	in cities with population over 500,000 1960	1980
South Korea	28	55	35	41	61	77
North Korea	40	60	15	12	15	19
Brazil	46	65	14	16	35	52
Mexico	51	67	28	32	36	48
Non-OPEC middle-income countries	39	52	28	27	36	48
Developed countries	68	77	18	18	48	55

Source: World Bank, *World Development Report 1981*, 172–73.

national security. Moreover, location decisions based on regional favoritism result in an inefficient allocation of resources—that is, economic losses—as well. The motivation for regional favoritism has been the fear of losing political power. To ensure the loyalty of the armed forces and bureaucrats, President Park surrounded himself with generals, colonels, and high-ranking bureaucrats who were from his home region, and eliminated others from important positions. In consequence, other regions have lost advocates in the administration, which completely dominates the legislature. The same situation still prevails under President Chun, who rose to prominence within the army because of his loyalty to Park and because he came from Park's home region.

Solutions

Interregional imbalance is evidence that all groups are not given equal opportunity for full participation in sharing the benefits of economic growth. Since the problem originates from the lack of local autonomy and from dictatorship backed by the military and the bureaucracy, democracy is the most important part of the solution. No democratic government will be able to favor one region and discriminate against others in a homogeneous country like Korea, where no region enjoys a commanding advantage in population size. Even during the dictatorial government of President Rhee, regional discrimination did not exist. Once it had been set in motion by President Park, however there was no turning back. Chun may not have wanted to continue Park's regionalistic policy, but his survival depends on the support of the privileged and powerful group from his home region, and thus he has no alternative but to continue favoring this region. Local autonomy based on the principle of home rule will also lessen the importance of Seoul and thus improve the balance among regions. Koreans did enjoy home rule from 1952 to 1961, but since then Presidents Park and Chun have wanted complete control over all levels of the government. Restoration of democracy would permit durable home rule in Korea and thus would slow, if not reverse, the trend of concentration into Seoul.

Although democracy and home rule will go far toward promoting a more balanced regional development, improvement of the quality of education in the rest of the country will also contribute significantly to this objective. Universities and high schools in Seoul are much superior to those in other cities, which in turn are superior to those in the rural areas. Many Korean parents, therefore, move to Seoul for the purpose of giving better educations to their children, even if it means substantial financial sacrifices. A balanced education policy aimed at improving the quality of education in the rural areas and small cities would not only reduce interregional imbalances but also promote a more equitable distribution of human capital and hence a more equitable distribution of income.

In 1971, as a presidential candidate, I proposed relocation of the nation's capital city from Seoul to Tae-jun. The population of Seoul was then about four million, and has swelled to nearly ten million by now. Had my proposal been adopted then, Seoul would not have grown so rapidly. In addition to relocation of the capital, dispersion of many of the central government agencies to other cities would also promote a more balanced regional development. There is no good reason for every agency to be located in Seoul. The country itself is small, and with the recent development of communication and transportation technologies, dispersion of government agencies will not hamper their coordinated functioning.

Intersectoral imbalances

Imbalance between rural and urban economies

In the process of economic development, it is natural for rural population to decline both relatively and absolutely, while urban population grows faster than the overall population. Thus, the decline of Korea's farm population is not in itself an evidence of rural impoverishment. Nevertheless, rural impoverishment will accelerate the flight of rural households into urban centers and create serious social problems. Many Korean farm households want to sell their properties to pay off their debts but, because of the impoverishment of the rural economy, there are no buyers. Unable to liquidate their properties, millions of farm households have abandoned their homes and farms, and fled to urban centers (mostly Seoul) in order to avoid

debt burdens that were becoming heavier each year and to find better opportunities for themselves and their children.[2]

The plight of Korea's farmers has been the main cause of their flight
to the cities. During the period 1965–75, Korea's farm population declined
at an average annual rate of 1.77 percent, while total population increased
by 2.08 percent per year. The rate of decrease in farm population since
1975 has accelerated to 3.08 percent per year while total population was
growing at 1.55 percent per year.[3] Farm population accounted for 55.1
percent of total population in 1965 and 24.6 percent in 1982.

Table 7-2 shows that an increasing proportion of farm households have
become indebted; moreover, debts are growing faster than incomes. If greater
indebtedness were due to a rapid increase in debt-financed investment, rising
debt burdens would not necessarily mean impoverishment of farmers. That,
however, is not the situation of Korean farmers. For example, average debt
per farm household rose by 54.9 percent in 1983, in contrast to a 12.5
percent increase in nominal GNP. Moreover, borrowing for subsistence expenditures rose by 147.4 percent, and other consumption expenditures have
also significantly contributed to the indebtedness of farm households. As a
result, only 61.3 percent of the debt increments was used for investment
and other farm expenses.[4]

One of the main causes of rural impoverishment has been deterioration
of the terms of trade, a ratio of the index of prices received by farmers to
the price index of purchases by farm households. As shown in Table 7-2,
the terms of trade, which peaked at 108.1 in 1973, have steadily declined
during the second half of the 1970s and dropped precipitously since 1980.
Such deterioration of the terms of trade not only reduces farmers' incomes
relative to those of others, but also acts as a disincentive for farming and
thus accelerates the abandonment of farming.

Table 7-2. Indicators of the farm economy

Year	1971	1978	1980	1982	1983
Indebted farm households (percent of total)	75.7%	85.3%	85.6%	87.3%	89.6%
Debt increase (percent of income)	n.a.	5.9	12.6	18.6	n.a.
Terms of trade[a]	100.0	105.0	100.0	94.8	84.9

Source: Bank of Korea, Economic Statistics Yearbook, 1983, and various official statistics as
    reported in Dong-A Ilbo, 10 August 1983, 18 April 1984, 22 April 1984, and Dae-
    Han Daily News, 19 March 1984.
a. Defined as the ratio of the index of prices received by farmers to the price index
    of the farm households' purchases. Base year is 1980.

Another major cause of rural impoverishment is the unfair taxation policy.[5] First, Korea's farmers pay taxes on gross income rather than net income. They are not allowed to deduct their expenses on seeds, fertilizer, herbicides and insecticides, farm equipment maintenance and repair, and so on from their taxable incomes. Such an unfair taxation policy severely disadvantages farmers relative to urban wage-earners.

Second, basic deductions are also unfair to the farmers. For an urban wage-earning family of five (average family size), the basic deduction from taxable income is 2,852 thousand won, compared with only 1,150 thousand won for a farm household in a similar economic situation.

Third, tax rates are also unfair to the farmers. The marginal tax rates on farm incomes are 6 percent up to 150 thousand won, 8 percent for incomes from 150 thousand to 300 thousand won, and 10 percent for over 300 thousand won. In contrast, the marginal tax rates on wage incomes are 6 percent up to 1.2 million won and 7 percent for incomes from 1.2 million to 1.8 million won.

The effects of these tax disadvantages of farming are such that, while an urban wage-earning family of five with an annual income of 3.6 million won ($4,500) pays 43,200 won for the labor-income tax (an effective tax rate of 1.2 percent), a farm household of the same size making the same amount of income must pay 388,800 won (an effective tax rate of 10.8 percent) for the farm-income tax. Thus, Korea's farmers find little incentive to continue farming, since it carries enormous tax disadvantages.

In addition to the deterioration of the terms of trade and tax disadvantages, the low-technology, low-wage bias of the industrial policy has created a skewed labor market, in which the unemployment rate for the less-educated workers is much lower than that for the well educated (see Table 6-2), and has encouraged many young people and middle-age men to abandon rural areas. The result is that most of Korea's farms are now operated by middle-age women and old couples. This combination of disincentive and low-productivity farmers led to the recent output declines in major crops.

Korea's rice production has grown at an average annual rate of only 2.2 percent since 1973, compared with a 15.9 percent annual growth rate for industrial production (see Table 7-3). Because rice is the most important crop in Korea, accounting for about 60 percent of cultivated area and about the same fraction of farm income, the decline of rice production since 1977 and the deterioration of its relative price have further worsened farm incomes since the reduction in rice production has not been offset by increases in the production of other major crops. Between 1977 and 1982, real GNP originating from agriculture and forestry increased by only 0.26 percent per year, while total GNP rose by 4.53 percent per year. Over a longer period of time, 1962–82, agriculture and forestry output grew by 3.45 percent per year, compared with 8.90 percent for total GNP.[6] This is in sharp contrast with the Chinese economy's recent record of balanced growth. There, ag-

to encourage farming. Equalizing the tax burdens of farmers and wage-earners is therefore the least Korea's government can do for the farmers.

To reverse the recent negative trends in rice production and farm incomes, a major change in price policy and investment allocation is called for. An emphasis on increasing agricultural output by investing in agricultural research and development and capital formation requires a shift away from the bias in investment allocation that has favored industry over agriculture.[8] The rapid increase in rice production in the mid-1970s was due to wide adoption of a new high-yield variety. Accelerated research and development of better varieties can make self-sufficiency possible, as Japan and Taiwan have demonstrated.

Agricultural price policy is a critical issue in Korea's farm economy. The current price policy calls for government purchases of rice and barley at prices higher than the prices of sales to urban consumers. The objective of this policy is to provide price incentives to farmers while retail prices are kept low for the urban consumers. In the process, however, the government subsidizes *all* consumers regardless of their needs and thus incurs unnecessarily large budget deficits. The deficits in turn limit the government's ability to maintain high purchase prices and thus reduce the efficacy of price incentives.

There is no need to subsidize all consumers. By limiting the subsidy to the truly needy, budget deficits can be substantially reduced. I propose a simple program of grain stamps, similar to food stamps in the United States, to be made available to needy families to meet their basic diet requirements. The government-held grains will be auctioned off to private grain dealers, and the retail prices of grains will then be determined by supply and demand. The government purchase price of rice will be determined by the long-run price elasticity of supply in order to ensure long-run self-sufficiency in rice. No price support for other grains is necessary since it is economically inefficient.[9]

The Agricultural Cooperative, Irrigation Cooperative, and Land Improvement Cooperative have been important vehicles of the government's agricultural policy. While these institutions have served useful functions, their undemocratic management has also contributed to the plight of farmers. These are cooperatives in name but not in reality, since all officers have been appointed and administrative directives are handed down from above.[10] Too often, the executives in Seoul look after the interests of big businesses (e.g., tying in unnecessarily large quantities of fertilizers with farm credits) at the expense of those of farmers. Democratic management of these cooperatives by officers elected by farmers will enhance the interests of all farmers and prevent the abuses designed to benefit big businesses.

Finally, farm economy can be improved by promoting an increased industrial use of agricultural output. For reasons to be discussed shortly, Korea's manufacturers are currently better off importing their material inputs rather than buying from domestic suppliers. Removal of artificial incentives to use imports will increase the industrial use of domestic agricultural output and thus promote a more balanced growth of the agricultural and industrial sectors of the economy.

Interindustrial imbalance

Whether a developing country should pursue a strategy of balanced economic development or an unbalanced development is a matter of dispute. There is no doubt, however, that the ultimate goal is balanced development. An unbalanced development is only a short-run strategy aimed at maximizing the efficiency of limited resources. Although I advocated balanced development for Korea in the 1960s, that is now a bygone issue. By the mid-1970s, however, Korea's economy had reached a stage where balancing of the previously unbalanced growth would have resulted in a more robust economic structure.

As I have shown in Chapter 4, Korea's economy is excessively dependent on foreign trade because of its failure to expand domestic markets. This failure, in turn, has been the result of the government's conscious policy of promoting exports of outputs and imports of material inputs and plants. In addition, concentration of income and wealth has weakened the purchasing power of workers and farmers and thus contributed to the failure to expand domestic markets. Furthermore, an ambitious but ill-advised plan of President Park (subsequently adhered to by President Chun) to dedicate most of the resources to the development of heavy and chemical industries resulted in an even greater imbalance at the time when increased balance was needed.[11]

Most of all, various incentives aimed at promoting exports, such as tax credits, subsidies, and low-interest financing, have inflicted penalties, relatively, on industries selling in domestic markets. These industries have had to compete against imports while contending with financial obstacles resulting from the government's steering of funds toward the export sector. There was another twist in the export promotion policy: imports of plants, raw material, and intermediate inputs for production of export commodities have been exempted from various taxes, but all domestic suppliers are subject to taxes. As a result, manufacturers have avoided using domestic supplies, preferring imports. This is why Korea's shipbuilding industry, the world's second-largest, has been dependent on imported tools. Thus, blind pursuit of export growth has resulted in interindustrial distortions of serious proportions.

The weak link between the export sector and the domestic-market-oriented sector contributes to the trade deficits, since imported inputs are preferred to those available in domestic markets. For this reason, Korea's trade balance remained consistently negative during the past two decades when exports grew extremely rapidly. Since the Korean economy must rely on imports for certain capital goods, energy, and certain raw material, strengthening the interindustrial linkages among the export industries and the others will make it possible to use precious foreign exchange for more productive purposes.

Links between the large firms and the small or medium-sized firms are also weak. As previously pointed out, Korea's conglomerates are vertically integrated to a large degree in the production of a vast group of commodities. As a result, Korea's small or medium-sized firms and large firms are not complementary, as they are in, say, Japan. For example, while 60.7 percent of Japan's small or medium-sized firms received contracts from large concerns, the corresponding figure for Korea is only 18 percent.[12] The result is a strange form of dual economy, in which most of the manufactured goods and banking and financial services are supplied by monopolistic or oligopolistic firms, and small or medium-sized firms fight for the remaining small portion of the market.[13]

How to correct interindustrial imbalance

Interindustrial imbalance, like interregional imbalance, prevents some groups from sharing in the economic growth process. The solutions for the problem of interindustrial imbalance are very simple. Since these imbalances are created mainly by the government's market interventions, which have distorted market signals and incentives, restoring the proper function of the free market will solve most of the problems. In particular, the following government-induced distortions must be corrected.

First, government intervention in the financial market must be avoided. The misguided efforts to steer funds into particular sectors of the economy or to particular industries have resulted in inefficient allocation of resources and imbalances among sectors and among industries. Moreover, government pressures on banks to force them to lend to particular corporations must be stopped. Such a practice is fundamentally against the spirit of Mass-Participatory Economy.

Second, the discriminatory tax system ought to be reformed. A system of taxes and tariffs that encourages the use of imports in place of domestic supplies and various subsidy schemes for exports contribute to imbalances. These systems should be reformed so that exporters do not receive favorable treatment at the expense of other industries or firms. Export growth is beneficial to the economy but cannot in itself be the objective of economic policy. In my program for Mass-Participatory Economy, all production of goods, whether for export or for domestic markets, will be equally treated.

Third, the government must stop favoring bigger businesses over smaller ones, heavy industries over light industries, and capital-intensive plants over labor-intensive plants. In Korea, government attitudes have tremendous impacts on the real economy, and thus its misguided attitudes can lead to serious consequences. To avoid such consequences, the government should remain neutral and leave the outcome to the market.

Finally, almost all government or quasi-government enterprises should be made private, except where public management is absolutely necessary. These are, in reality, high-class welfare programs for retired generals and colonels, and serve no useful public purpose. Moreover, these enterprises have become hotbeds of corruption and collusion; as a result, they award contracts only to big businesses with clout and the ability to bribe, while smaller ones are shut out. Private management of these enterprises will not only increase management efficiency but also benefit small or medium-sized firms by giving them a chance to compete for contracts.

NOTES

1. *Dong-A Ilbo*, 23 December 1983.
2. For a documentary report on this phenomenon, see *Dong-A Ilbo*, 24 January 1984.
3. Bank of Korea, *Economic Statistics Yearbook*, various issues.
4. All statistics cited in this paragraph are obtained from the same sources used for Table 7-2.
5. The next four paragraphs are based on an article that appeared in *Dong-A Ilbo*, 24 May 1984.
6. Bank of Korea, *Economic Statistics Yearbook*, 1982 and 1983.
7. *New York Times*, 4 January 1984.
8. Since 1962, agriculture, forestry, and fisheries have received only 8.4 percent of total gross domestic capital formation. Since forestry and fisheries expanded very rapidly during this period, the share of agriculture is probably minuscule.
9. The government operation to reduce seasonal variations in grain prices will be abolished, and it is expected that this function will be better performed by private enterprises. There is no good reason why the government should be the price stabilizer.
10. Recent attempts to elect local officers will not change the characters of these cooperatives as long as the central executive body is appointed by the government under the control of a dictator.
11. Waste of precious foreign capital has also been great, for many of these industries subsequently had to be bailed out by the government.
12. *Dong-A Ilbo*, 15 June 1983.
13. See Chapter 5.

8

Monetary and fiscal policies

Financial system and monetary policy

In addition to the various types of imbalances discussed in the preceding chapter, there are two other prominent imbalances in Korea: (1) the imbalance between its financial system and the rest of the economy, and (2) the imbalance between the political system and the economic, cultural, and educational standards of the people. While the economic, cultural, and educational standards of Korea have improved significantly during the past four decades, the political system has become increasingly backward and the financial system has made very little progress, if any. The backwardness of the financial system has been primarily due to the backwardness of the political system.

The proof of the financial system's backwardness is the existence of an underground private loan market. Despite repeated government attempts to absorb it into the institutionalized financial system, the undergound loan market has persisted to this day, with little change in its relative importance. The main reason for the persistence of the underground loan market is government intervention in credit allocations and interest-rate determination. Because of the low profitability of banks and low interest rates on deposits, people with surplus funds avoid the banking system. In addition, many borrowers are unable to obtain credit from the banking system because of their lack of connections; they turn to the underground market, willing to pay higher interest rates.

Thus, government interventions tend to drive a wedge between the official interest rates and the black-market rates. As a result, the banking system is chronically short of funds, making the underground loan market indispensable. Even the ten largest conglomerates, which in 1982 received 20.8 percent of the banking system's total credit extension, have been estimated to rely on the underground market for nearly 15 percent of their total borrowing.[1] For smaller firms, the importance of the underground loan market is greater, and very small firms rely exclusively on this market. In fact, it is misleading to describe this market as "underground." Although it is unlawful and therefore lacks legal protection of its participants, this market is ubiquitous and fulfills the function that should be performed by the banking system.

The existence of dual banking markets has often been exploited by unscrupulous people with good connections. Borrowing from banks at the official rates of interest and then turning around to lend in the black market at higher interest rates is a very profitable business, if one has the ability to borrow.

The infamous Chang Young-Ja scandal of 1982 is a case in point. Chang, a relative of President Chun's wife, pressured the banks to lend her about $1 billion, which she in turn lent in the underground market. The whole scheme unraveled only because the scale of the operation was too large, and eventually several large corporations, which had been swindled out of hundreds of millions of dollars, went bankrupt. The ensuing disruption of the nation's financial system was the main reason for the slowdown of economic recovery from 6.4 percent real GNP growth in 1981 to 5.3 percent in 1982.

His image badly tarnished, President Chun attempted to divert the blame to the bank executives and Chang. As a part of that scheme, the government-owned commercial banks were to be auctioned off and privately managed. In a prearranged bidding, the government successfully sold its bank shares to a handful of large conglomerates. Thus, on paper, commercial banks are privately managed. In reality, however, bank managers follow the needs of the owner-conglomerates and the government's wishes. Most important of all, interest rates, except for very small variations within the narrow allowable ranges, are still determined by the government and credit allocation is subject to covert pressures of the administration.

Within the Korean banking industry, domestic banks have suffered from chronically poor rates of profit while foreign banks reap enormous profits. For example, the net income of the domestic commercial banks declined by 25 percent in 1983, while at the same time, foreign banks in Korea enjoyed phenomenal rates of return.[2] The difference in profitability is due to government interference and political pressure in the allocation of the loans of domestic commercial banks and to government control of interest rates.

One serious consequence of government control of the banking system has been the inability of the Bank of Korea to control the money supply. Because of political pressures, banks have had to make loans even when they could not meet the reserve requirements. As a result, the money supply tended to grow faster than the central bank intended, and the people have long suffered from double-digit inflation. Moreover, the existence of the underground loan market, though indispensable to the economy, has made it difficult for the central bank to gauge monetary statistics and evaluate its monetary policy.

The solution to the problems of the financial system is, as in other areas, to avoid government interventions and to let the market function freely. Intervention in financial markets seriously limits some groups' opportunity to participate in the economic growth process. There is no good reason to make the private loan market unlawful. Legitimizing this useful market activity and eschewing government interference in interest-rate determination will have two healthy consequences. First, the loan interest rate will be reduced as premiums for possible penalty and uninsurable default risk will be eliminated; second, bank deposit interest rates will be increased above the artificially low official rates and thus encourage savings. In addition, truly free management of banks without undue influence of conglomerates will eventually integrate the underground loan market into the institutional banking system. As long as the banking system remains subject to government intervention, the Korean economic system will be a limping free-market system. A free-banking system, on the other hand, will correct many of the concentration and imbalance problems discussed in the previous sections. Once again, it must be recognized that a genuinely free banking system cannot be achieved under dictatorship since, by their very nature, dictatorial governments will make banking decisions subject to their own will.

Fiscal policy

We have already discussed the serious repercussions of a tax system aimed at promoting exports. At a broader level, Korea's fiscal system is defective for three reasons: (1) the tax structure is extremely regressive; (2) the tax burden is excessively high; and (3) expenditures are wasteful.

Korea's tax system relies heavily on regressive indirect taxes; in 1982, 72 percent of total tax revenues came from indirect taxes. In contrast, the corresponding figures for the same year were 26.6 percent in the United States and 27.6 percent in Japan. In addition, arbitrary tax assessments impose heavier burdens on the small or medium-sized firms than on the large firms. For example, the government lost 71.6 percent of the tax cases appealed to the tax court in 1983.[3] Since large corporations did not appeal to the tax court, one can be justified in concluding that arbitrary assessments tend to be biased against small businesses. The handling of the 1977 introduction of the value-added tax further illustrates the government's arbitrariness. In order to implement this tax, all small stores were told to buy cash registers (not an inexpensive item for them); then, however, the government refused to accept the registered sales totals.[4]

Korea's tax burden, at 20.6 percent of GNP for the fiscal year 1984, may not seem excessive. However, if various forms of hidden taxes and poor government services are considered, the burden exceeds those of the developed countries.[5] The hidden taxes are, for example, contributions (more or less forced) to the Defense Fund and emergency relief funds, political contributions, and various forms of fees.

In exchange for these burdensome taxes, the Korean people get poor government services. As shown in Table 8-1, too much of Korea's government expenditures are devoted to defense and, compared with other middle-income countries, the government provides relatively unfavorable educa-

Table 8-1. International comparison of government budget composition

| Country | Defense expenditures as percent of: | | | | Central government expenditures per capita (1975 dollars): | | | | | |
| | GNP | | Central government expenditures | | Defense | | Education | | Health | |
	1972	1978	1972	1978	1972	1978	1972	1978	1972	1978
Korea	4.9%	6.3%	25.8%	38.0%	$22	$49	$14	$21	$1	$2
Singapore	6.0	5.4	35.3	26.8	126	164	56	88	28	52
Brazil	1.4	1.1	8.3	5.8	13	14	11	14	10	20
Mexico	0.6	0.6	4.9	3.4	8	8	27	47	8	9
Non-OPEC middle-income countries	2.8	2.9	12.6	12.6	24	32	20	34	9	20
Developed countries	5.1	2.9	21.6	13.4	301	281	80	120	152	229

Source: World Bank, World Development Report 1981, 180–81.

tional services and very few health services.[6] Moreover, an increasingly large portion of defense and nondefense expenditures are diverted to wasteful and destructive activities in order to maintain the unpopular dictatorial government. It has been reported that the number of government-hired thugs on campuses ready to break up student demonstrations was close to the number of students.[7] Seoul's newspapers have recently reported that the "diversion" of police to "other" duties (i.e., suppressing student demonstrations) invited a wave of violent crimes. As a result, crime-prevention industries (e.g., security guard services, locksmiths) are said to be rapidly growing.[8] Emergency transfer of police from other cities proved disastrous because so many of them did not know their newly assigned areas.

Most of all, defense expenditures to pay for the regimentation of the population divert precious resources from productive uses. Citizens' periodic civil-defense duties and reserve-army duties not only cost the government money to run the programs but also too frequently disrupt economic activities. Since defense and police-related expenditures claim about one-half of total expenditures, and since a large portion of these expenditures is spent to maintain a police-state, a significant part of the total expenditures are diverted from other uses.[9] This is why Koreans pay heavy taxes but get so few government services in education, health, and social welfare and no social security.

Another element in Korea's tax burden is heavy development expenditures, which have been necessitated by the low personal saving rate.[10] To make up for the shortfall in national investment, the government has been relying heavily on public saving. Still another factor is the propensity of the government to assume an unnecessarily large role in the national economy. By promoting a higher personal saving rate through interest-rate deregulation, luxury taxes, and a progressive consumption tax, Korea's dependence on the public sector for development expenditures can be, and should be, reduced.

The above discussion suggests the following measures for a more efficient fiscal policy. First, in order to spread the tax burden more equitably, the regressive tax system ought to be replaced by a progressive tax system. This can be done by replacing the value-added tax with a progressive consumption tax.[11] Unlike a progressive income tax, which has a negative work incentive if it is too progressive, a consumption tax encourages saving; the more progressive the tax system, the greater the incentive to save. Thus, this tax will not only make the system fairer, but also increase the personal saving rate, relieving the government of the burden of development expenditures. This relief in turn will make it possible for the government to increase badly needed expenditures on education, research and development, health, and social welfare.

Second, eliminating wasteful defense and police-related expenditures will free resources for other uses without weakening Korea's defense capabilities. In order to accomplish this, however, Korea must first regain democracy. Only a democratic government could afford to eliminate these expenditures. A democratic government would not need to increase tension and create border infractions to justify suppression, and it would not need to flood college campuses with thugs and police. To the contrary, it would be under pressure to reduce tension and promote peaceful exchange with North Korea and strive for peaceful reunification. Moreover, institution of democratic political processes will enhance the Korean people's resolve to defend and preserve their freedom. There is only one sure way to maintain national *security*: give the people *something to secure*—that is, freedom and prosperity.

NOTES

1. Ministry of Finance's report to the National Assembly (as reported in *Dong-A Ilbo*, 11 November 1983).
2. For example, Bank of America reaped net income that was 3.7 times its capital, and several others had rates of return of 45 to 90 percent! See *Dae-Han Daily News*, 6 March 1984; *Dong-A Ilbo*, 21 February 1984.
3. *Dong-A Ilbo*, 20 January 1984.
4. Park Chan-Jong, *Shameful Stories* (quoted from *Dae-Han Daily News*, 31 January 1984). Park Chan-Jong was an influential member of the Park Chung Hee government.

5. This was the conclusion of a research paper quoted, but not clearly identified, in *Dong-A Ilbo*, 20 January 1984.
6. Public education and health services are the responsibility of the central government in Korea.
7. *Asahi Shimbun*, 20 April 1983.
8. *Dae-Han Daily News*, 8 May 1984.
9. Accurate accounting is impossible because numerous expenditure items are hidden in the budgets of other ministries.
10. See Chapter 4.
11. The degree of progressivity may depend on the absolute amount of consumption, the percentage of income consumed, or some combination. Tax rates can also be used as a tool of macroeconomic policy.

9

Education and social welfare policy

As discussed in the preceding chapter, government expenditures for
education and social welfare in Korea are relatively low compared with those
of other middle-income developing countries. The crucial role of education
in economic development has been pointed out in Chapter 2. Equally important for social stability, and thus for economic development, is the provision of basic social services for the poor, the disabled, the disadvantaged,
and senior citizens.

Education policy

Korean parents have a fervent desire to educate their children, as
suggested by the statistics shown in Table 9-1. The primary-school enrollment ratio, which was 94 percent in 1960, rose to 111 percent in 1978,
indicating that many adults were enrolled in the primary-school programs.
The secondary-school enrollment ratio rose even more dramatically, from
27 percent in 1960 to 74 percent, comparing favorably with those of other
developing countries. If Korea's low dropout rate is taken into account, the
secondary-school graduation ratio is likely to be closer to those of the developed countries than the enrollment ratios indicate. The higher-education
enrollment ratio has more than doubled from 5 percent in 1960 to 11 percent
in 1977, but was somewhat lower than the average for the non-OPEC middle-
income countries. It appears that other developing countries have put relatively greater emphasis on higher education and less on the primary and
secondary levels than the Asian NICs have. This difference may have played
an important role in the relatively superior economic growth rates and
income distributions of the Asian NICs.

The statistics shown in Table 9-1 are thus very encouraging. However,
according to the data presented in Table 8-1, the Korean government's
education expenditures were generally smaller than those of other developing
countries in terms of both absolute dollars per capita and percentage of total
budget. The seeming discrepancy between the high enrollment ratio and
low government expenditures is the result of large expenditures by the
parents. In Korea only elementary schools are free of tuition. Although
tuitions of public high schools are lower than those of private schools,
financial burdens on parents are quite heavy. Moreover, college tuitions are
many times more expensive than high-school tuitions. Nevertheless, com-

71

Table 9-1. International comparison of school enrollment ratios and
adult literacy rates

Enrollment ratio (percent of relevant age group)

Country	Primary school		Secondary school		Higher education[a]		Adult literacy (percent of total)	
	1960	1978	1960	1978	1960	1977	1960	1976
Korea	94%	111%	27%	74%	5%	11%	71%	93%
Hong Kong	87	115	20	57	4	10	70	90
Singapore	111	109	32	57	6	9	n.a.	83[b]
Brazil	95	88	11	24	2	13	61	76
Mexico	80	116	11	39	3	11	65	82
Middle-income countries	87	97	19	44	5	13	62	76
Developed countries	114	100	68	89	17	37	n.a.	99

Source: World Bank, World Development Report 1981, 178–79.
a. College-age is defined as 20 to 24 years of age.
b. 1980 figure.

petition for college admission is so tough that many good students fail to gain admission. But for the lack of facilities and professors, annual college admissions could easily be doubled or tripled.

The inadequacy of the Korean government's educational expenditures is reflected in student/teacher ratios. As shown in Table 9-2, these ratios in Korea are significantly higher than the averages for the low-income developing countries. Thus, Korea's relatively high enrollment ratios have been achieved by crowding the classrooms and by increasing the workload of teachers.[1] Moreover, the student/teacher ratio in secondary schools has increased in Korea since 1960, while it has decreased in the low-income and developed countries. Since Korea's ratio is over 90 percent higher than the average ratio for developing countries, a continuation of the upward trend should not be tolerated.

The student/teacher ratio for four-year colleges in Korea is also clearly too high. The most recent estimate, 34.4 in 1983, is close to the corresponding figure for Korea's secondary schools and more than 70 percent higher than the average ratios for secondary schools in other developing countries. To make matters worse, the quality of higher education in Korea has suffered from the mandatory dismissal system introduced in 1981. According to this system, universities must admit 130 percent of the government-approved

Table 9-2. Comparison of student/teacher ratios

	1960	1970	Most recent estimate[a]
Korea			
Elementary	58.0	57.0	46.0
Secondary	34.0	37.0	39.0
Four-year colleges	n.a.	18.8	34.4
Low-income countries			
Elementary	44.7	41.8	35.6
Secondary	21.8	21.6	19.0
Non-OPEC middle-income countries			
Elementary	37.2	34.7	31.9
Secondary	17.2	19.7	20.9
Developed countries			
Elementary	31.1	24.2	20.2
Secondary	19.8	17.8	14.4

Source: World Bank, World Tables, 3d ed., vol. 2; Korean Council of Higher Education (as reported in Dong-A Ilbo, 7 April 1984).
a. College-age is defined as 20 to 24 years of age.
b. 1980 figure.

quota but 30 percent must be dismissed before graduation, *regardless of their records*. This cruel system was designed to make students so preoccupied with survival that they would not participate in demonstrations and other political or social activities. This system has been severely criticized, and a recent research paper concluded that it has contributed to a decline in the quality of higher education.[2] The government finally relented in 1984 and decided to abolish the system.

Korea's higher education has also been suffering from constant disruptions and frequent dismissals of professors for political reasons. As discussed in Chapter 3, Korea's colleges and universities have been the battlegrounds for democracy, human rights, and academic freedom since 1960. If the total cost of these disruptions could be measured, the cumulative losses over the past quarter-century would be astronomical.

Restoration of democracy would remove many barriers to quality higher education. First, there would be no disruptions of learning or dismissals of students and professors for political reasons; many excellent professors who have been dismissed would return to campuses and relieve the shortage of professors. Second, the enormous government expenditures now needed to support political terrorism, both official and unofficial, of the police, military, and hired thugs and to maintain ubiquitous intelligence networks could be diverted to improve the nation's education system.

A democratic government, however, should not wait passively for such improvements. Rather, it must actively push for improved services in education, recognizing that, as discussed in Chapter 2, Korea's best resource is its human capital. Moreover, in order for all groups to participate meaningfully in the development process, it is essential that Korea's citizens be well educated and well informed. Therefore, the development of manpower (not in the narrow sense of goods-producing power but in the broad sense of the whole character of a person), together with national defense, must be treated as the nation's highest priority. Specific recommendations are discussed below.

First, secondary-level education must be made free and compulsory as early as possible. To this end, free education up to the ninth-grade level should be offered immediately. There is no reason why Korea cannot offer this; Taiwan has been able to do so since the early 1960s. I believe free education up to the twelfth-grade level is within reach if the Korean government is willing to eliminate unnecessary expenditures as discussed in the preceding chapter.

Second, the pupil/teacher ratio at the elementary level must be lowered immediately. It is important that elementary-school children be given adequate attention by teachers, since childhood learning habits have a lasting influence into adulthood.

Third, teachers at all levels of education must be respected and remunerated accordingly. It is widely known that school teachers in Japan are well paid and thus Japanese schools have no shortage of good teachers. Korean teachers, in contrast, are underpaid and do not enjoy the respect of society as they once did. Moreover, college professors have been ordered by the Ministry of Education to prevent student demonstrations, and administrators of higher-educational institutions have frequently been pressured into resignation because of their failure to prevent demonstrations. As a result of inadequate compensation and lack of respect, many good teachers in Korea have left the profession. To improve the quality of teachers at all levels and to lower the pupil/teacher ratio at the elementary level, teachers' salaries must be raised to socially respectable levels.

Fourth, private participation in the provision of higher education must be encouraged. As pointed out earlier, much of the Koreans' educational attainment has been made possible by *enterprising* private institutions. Many founders of these institutions make profits by unlawful means from the schools they founded. To prevent such abuses and to encourage private investment in educational institutions, I propose tax preferences that I believe will reduce the incentive for unlawful profit-making.

Fifth, to increase the quality of higher education, colleges and universities must be given full autonomy within broad guidelines consistent with the nation's education policy. Under the current system, all colleges and universities are tightly controlled by the central government, which allows them no authority for experimentation. Under such circumstances, Korea's higher-education system would be unable to adapt promptly to changing needs. To further assure flexibility, academic freedom must be vigorously protected. In a world where technologies are becoming increasingly sophisticated, and social, national, and international problems increasingly complex, academic freedom is essential if new and timely ideas are to be developed.

Sixth, international student exchanges must be encouraged. Such exchanges help Korean citizens understand other cultures and also help foreigners understand Korea better. It is imperative that nations understand each other in order to function competently in this increasingly interdependent world. Moreover, enhanced mutual understanding among nations would increase the probability of avoiding a catastrophic nuclear war.

Seventh, equal opportunity for secondary and higher education must be provided for adults with full-time occupations. The present Korean system gives virtually no second chance to those who have "missed their trains." This is an unwise policy, given the importance of education to nation building. My goal is to increase opportunities for higher education for everyone, so that over 50 percent of adult Koreans will eventually attain higher education.

Last but not least, the government must ensure that educational attainment is not determined by the financial ability of the parents but by the academic prowess of the students.

Social welfare policy

President Chun proclaimed in 1981 his goal of leading the country into a "New Welfare State." He promised to enact social security and health insurance and to construct many waste-water treatment plants, among other things.[3] Not long after the plan was announced, however, the social security plan was shelved, and no one knows when sewage plants will be constructed, if ever. Limited health insurance policies are being handed out to the members of Chun's party.

As has been repeatedly emphasized throughout this book, economic *growth* alone does not bring about economic *development*. If any group does not share in the fruits of economic growth, development is deficient. Therefore, to ensure equal opportunity for full participation of all groups, society has an obligation to provide basic necessities to those who cannot secure them independently. These people include the disabled, the disadvantaged, and the temporarily unemployed. However, in fulfilling this obligation, society must make sure that the recipients of its generosity do not neglect their obligation to the society. Indeed the requirement of social responsibility on the part of recipients benefits the recipients themselves. Nothing is more destructive to human character than the feeling of worthlessness or the

Table 9-3. International comparison of health-related indicators

Country	Population per physician		Population per nursing person^a		Infant mortality rate^b	Life expectancy
	1960	MRE^c	1960	MRE^c	MRE^c	MRE^c
Korea	3,540	1,690	3,250	380	33.1	66.1
Hong Kong	3,060	1,220	2,880	790	9.8	75.0
Singapore	2,336	1,150	650	320	11.5	71.8
Mexico	1,830	1,260	3,650	1,420	54.4	65.6
Brazil	2,670	1,510	2,810	820	75.4	63.6
Argentina	740	420	750	580	44.4	70.9
United States	750	520	n.a.	140	11.7	75.0

Source: World Bank, *World Tables,* 3d ed., vol. 2.
a. Practicing graduate, practical, and assistant nurses. Definitions of nursing person may differ among countries.
b. Annual number of deaths of infants less than one year old per thousand live births.
c. Most recent estimate (1979 to 1981).

attitude of dependency. Furthermore, social welfare policy should not be limited to public handouts but must include educational opportunities to improve a person's whole character throughout his or her life.

The Korean government's expenditures for health services are negligible (see Table 8-1). It is not surprising, therefore, that Korea has a lower life expectancy and a higher infant-mortality rate than either Hong Kong or Singapore (see Table 9-3). The number of people per physician is also larger in Korea than in other NICS. Korea has exported a large number of physicians (about five thousand) to the United States, where they are less desperately wanted than at home; it is urgent that this physician drain be prevented. Needless to say, the lack of individual freedom has been an important factor in the massive emigration of physicians. Restoration of democracy and greater effort in health services are therefore urgently needed.

As for environmental policy, the government has not only been powerless to stop illegal dumping of wastes by big businesses, but has sometimes intimidated people who advocate environmental protection. To Presidents Park and Chun, economic growth has been an urgent priority for political reasons, and the long-run environmental consequences have been disregarded. Unfortunately, the price of past neglect cannot be avoided, and Koreans have begun to pay for it. According to a recent report by the Office of Environmental Protection, the air-pollution level in Seoul (0.051 parts per million of sulfur dioxide in 1983) was many times higher than those of other major cities of the world.[4] Moreover, municipal water in Seoul is so polluted that it looks rusty and is not potable. People drink it after boiling it, but it still contains chemical pollutants. I am afraid that in the long run many residents may become afflicted with cancer or other pollution-related diseases.

The important reason for the neglect of the environment is the lack of freedom of speech and the lack of political checks and balances—that is, the dictatorship. While *some* sacrifice in environment must be tolerated for the sake of improving living standards, the extent of environmental damage is too large to be ignored any longer. However, there is no effective political means available to the citizenry to pressure the government into responsible environmental policy. Furthermore, because of the collaboration between the government and big business, applications of environmental laws and regulations have become arbitrary. For example, it has recently been discovered that several large corporations have been illegally dumping untreated waste water into the Kum-Ho River.[5] The government announced that it would levy fines on these firms, but as usual nothing has been done since the announcement. At the same time, a small garment factory that was operating with forty sewing machines was indicted for exceeding the noise-level standard. The latter incident was reported in a newspaper column under the heading "the grievance of a small fish."[6]

There is a growing awareness of the problem of pollution among the Korean people, and the government must change its basic attitude. However, as long as one man's preference is forced on the people, the environmental problem cannot be resolved, for the task of preserving and cleaning the environment requires the voluntary participation of the people. The revival of the Thames could not have been accomplished without the voluntary participation of the British people. The same will be required of the Korean people to revive the Han River. As has been demonstrated in the United Kingdom, democracy would make it easy for the Korean people to participate voluntarily in this important task.

NOTES

1. The student/teacher ratio may not in itself be a good indicator of the quality of education, but it is a good indicator of many other variables reflecting government services in education.
2. Korean Council of Higher Education, "Higher Education's Contribution to the Development of the Nation," April 1984 (monograph).
3. Democratic Justice Party, *A Design for the New Welfare State* (Seoul, 1981).
4. See *Dong-A Ilbo*, 25 August 1984. According to the report, the sulfur dioxide levels in the atmospheres of other major cites are: 0.016–0.02 ppm in Tokyo (1981), 0.014 ppm in Osaka (1982), 0.018 ppm in New York (1978), and 0.009 ppm in Los Angeles (1978).
5. *Dong-A Ilbo*, 22 April 1984.
6. *Dong-A Ilbo*, 3 May 1984.

10

Conclusions

The preceding chapters have systematically reviewed the state of the Korean economy and proposed various policy measures. The guiding principle of these proposals is to strike a proper balance among the three major goals of growth, equality, and price stability. The goal of growth, in turn, is to be accomplished through a balanced development of various sectors and regions of the economy. To achieve this balance, full participation of all groups—entrepreneurs, workers, farmers, consumers, and so on—in various aspects of economic decision making must be assured under a democratic government.

My economic development program, based on participation of the masses, should not be confused with a socialistic development program. I emphatically reject socialism. Either partial or complete state ownership of the means of production inevitably leads to inefficiencies, invites corruption, and increases the likelihood of dictatorship. Moreover, a mass-participatory economy becomes meaningless without individual responsibility and creativity. It is my belief that socialism is not conducive to individual creativity and responsibility.

However, my rejection of socialism does not imply an uncritical endorsement of capitalistic development to the neglect of individual rights and social justice. I am fundamentally against the kind of economic policy that has been practiced by the Park and Chun regimes, which treats workers and farmers as instruments of production and completely ignores social justice. Instead of the inhumane and coercive policies aimed at squeezing out the workers' maximum efforts without giving them adequate compensation and wholesome and safe workplaces, my program advocates a vigorous upholding of the workers' rights in order to ensure their participation with creativity and responsibility. Similarly, measures are proposed to reduce the gaps between the urban and the rural economies and between the rich and the poor.

Maximum reliance on the market is the operating principle of my program. As has been shown throughout this book, most of the economic problems in Korea resulted from the government's unnecessary interventions in the market functions. It is argued that dictatorship has been responsible for most of these market interventions, since, by its very nature, a dictatorial government tends to exercise excessive authority over many areas where it should not be involved. Restoration of democracy and market functions free of government interferences, therefore, is the key to the solutions of most of these problems.

The most serious government interventions have been in foreign trade, the labor market, and credit allocation. The Korean government has richly earned its reputation for unfair trade practices. In its misguided effort to promote exports and discourage imports, various export incentives have been bestowed on export industries, and many nontariff import barriers have been applied. Thus, Korea's exporters are accused of dumping in foreign markets while domestic consumers pay exhorbitant prices. At the same time, the government publicly humiliates people who get caught for smoking foreign cigarettes, and civil servants are paranoid about inadvertently using any foreign-made goods, for discovery would cost them their jobs. This practice must be stopped. Free trade promotes efficiency and provides the best consumer protection. Furthermore, I believe that free trade and free international flow of capital affords a possibility of world integration and thus world survival.

Government interventions in the labor market have been so consistently against labor that they are accurately described as an anti-labor, low-wage policy. The economic and social consequences of such a policy are the slowdown of productivity growth, widening of the gap between the rich and the poor, social unrest, and polarization of the nation. Instead of the ill-advised policy of imposing unilateral sacrifices on labor, my program advocates a goverment role as impartial arbitrator in labor–management disputes and as a protector of the rights of all groups, particularly those of workers.

Much of Korea's interindustrial imbalance and market concentration is attributable to government intervention in credit allocation. Moreover, as a result of such intervention, domestic financial institutions have been unprofitable, while foreign banks reap huge profits. One important measure of the inefficiency of domestic financial institutions is the existence of an underground private loan market. Without this underground loan market the Korean economy would collapse, since most households and business firms rely on this market to a greater extent than they do on the public financial institutions.

To promote more efficient and balanced industrial development, financial institutions must be given the freedom to use their own judgment in credit allocation, and interest rates should be allowed to reflect financial market conditions. This will not only facilitate restoration of interindustrial balance but also increase the efficiency of the financial market itself by absorbing the underground loan market into the public financial institutions.

In addition to the above proposals, my program includes other policy measures designed to restore interregional balance, reduce the gap between the urban and rural economies, reform the regressive tax system, and provide for more efficient delivery of government services, particularly in education, health, and social welfare.

Interregional imbalance in the Korean economy has become a serious problem that threatens national unity. In a homogeneous country like Korea, there is no reason for such regional disparity in living standards and industrial development. The only reason for this imbalance has been regional discrimination by the Park and Chun regimes. Since regional discrimination has been used in order to ensure the loyalty of the military and the bureaucracy to Park and Chun, restoration of interregional balance rests on the restoration of democracy in Korea.

Similarly, the growing gap between the urban and rural economies stems from the government's disdain toward farmers, who have been slighted in order to placate urban consumers, and the neglect of agricultural investment. A democratic government would not and should not be permitted to neglect the rural economy.

Fiscal policy of the Park and Chun regimes has been characterized by an unfair tax system with poor government services relative to the heavy tax burden. The current tax system relies on regressive indirect taxes for over 70 percent of total tax revenues. This system could be made fairer by replacing indirect taxes by direct taxes, including a progressive consumption tax. Poor government services are attributable to waste and authoritarianism. Even worse, the taxpayers' money has been squandered to terrorize and discipline the entire nation for the purpose of maintaining an authoritarian government. A government that likes to rule over the people rather than to serve them cannot deliver the services that they want. On the other hand, a democratic government, by its very nature, will strive to deliver these services.

Education is the foundation of the national economy. Education enables the citizenry to participate meaningfully in the economic, political, social, and cultural development of the nation. For these reasons, a greater emphasis on education is proposed. My long-term policy goal is the attainment of higher education by over 50 percent of adult Koreans. In the more immediate future, I propose free and compulsory secondary education, for Korea is lagging far behind other nations—at least two decades behind Taiwan, for example.

Social welfare turns economic growth into meaningful economic development. I believe society has an obligation to provide basic necessities to the needy, whether they are disabled, disadvantaged, or temporarily unemployed. However, in fulfilling this obligation, society's compassion must be carefully balanced so that the recipients do not neglect their obligation to society. Indeed, the greatest benefit to the recipients themselves is this requirement of social responsibility. Nothing is so destructive to human character as the feeling of worthlessness that attends an inability to work, whether through handicap or unemployment.

These proposals are my democratic alternatives to the policies of Park Chung Hee and Chun Doo Hwan. Under Park and Chun, the fruits of Korea's economic growth have been nearly monopolized by the privileged few, and participation of the workers and farmers in sharing these fruits has been systematically denied. My program attempts not only to redress this unfairness by upholding the rights of all groups, but also to seek a balanced and robust economic development by guaranteeing equal opportunity to all.